when
Big Issues
HAPPEN TO
Little Girls

Other Books by Erin A. Munroe

The Everything Guide to Stepparenting

The Anxiety Workbook for Girls

when Big Issues HAPPEN TO Little Girls

How to Prepare, React, and Manage Your Emotions
So You Can Best Support Your Daughter

Erin A. Munroe, LMHC

Foreword by
Michele Borba, Ed.D.
author of *The Big Book of Parenting Solutions*

Health Communications, Inc.
Deerfield Beach, Florida

www.hcibooks.com

Library of Congress Cataloging-in-Publication Data

Munroe, Erin A.
   When big issues happen to little girls : how to prepare, react, and manage your own emotions so you can best support your daughter / by Erin A. Munroe.
      p.   cm.
   Includes bibliographical references and index.
   ISBN-13: 978-0-7573-1532-9
   ISBN-10: 0-7573-1532-1
   1. Girls—Psychology.   2. Teenage girls—Psychology.   3. Adolescence.
4. Parenting.   I. Title.
   HQ777.M86 2010
   649'.133019—dc22

                                                                    2010028588

Publisher: Health Communications, Inc.
         3201 S.W. 15th Street
         Deerfield Beach, FL 33442–8190

Cover photo ©Inmagine
Cover and interior design by Lawna Patterson Oldfield

This book is dedicated to parents,
guardians, and other caring adults
of little girls everywhere.
Every extra ounce of love and patience
you can find for your girls is
deeply appreciated, and worth
more than you will
ever know.

It's not only children who grow.
Parents do too. As much as we watch to see
what our children do with their lives, they are
watching us to see what we do with ours.
I can't tell my children to reach for the sun.
All I can do is reach for it, myself.

—JOYCE MAYNARD

CONTENTS

ACKNOWLEDGMENTS

There is no way I would have the confidence to write at all without the support of those who were there throughout my own big issues as a little girl. I will forever thank my high school guidance counselor, Mr. Anthony King, my incredible English professor, Helen Whall, my parents, my dear husband, my stepson, my son, my incredible dogs, Simon and Izzy, and my entire extended family and friends for just being awesomely supportive.

I would like to thank my agent, mentor, editor, and kindred soul, Janice Pieroni of Story Arts Management, my lovely and energetic editor at HCI, Michele Matrisciani, and Tonya Woodworth, of HCI, for answering my goofy questions. My professional supervisors and sanity savers, Andy Ward, LICSW and Ellen Sinnott, RNCS. My writing inspirations, Dan Shaughnessy and Clark Booth—two generous writers who didn't have to take the time to help an aspiring writer but did. Dr. Irene Levine for being supercool and becoming a great role model. Dr. Cynthia Green for being kind and inspiring. Liz Jorgensen, CADC, for being so totally cool and down to earth and knowing how to explain the brain in English. Steven Gross,

MSW at Project Joy, for his time and reminding me to accept the joy of the writing process and to spread joy wherever I can. Harriette Wimms, Ph.D., and Anne Townsend, Ph.D., of Mariposa's Child Success Programs for their time, insight, and understanding of children, families, and parents. Maura Burnett from Mariposa and Rolland Janairo from Project Joy for being superefficient and great.

FOREWORD

I recently heard a story about a woman who was so afraid of bugs that the thought of them would make her physically ill and cause her nightmares. If she ran into one, she would panic, freeze, and become nauseous. If a critter was spotted in her home, most times she would vacate until someone came home to find the bug and get rid of it. As the woman grew older, she realized her fear was becoming worse and that waiting for her husband to come home from work before she could re-enter her house was out of control and harmful to her well-being. But it wasn't until the birth of her daughter that she realized just how detrimental her fear was . . . to the emotional health of her child.

Upon an encounter with a palmetto bug (cockroach) in her laundry room, the Virginia native shrieked and jumped onto a step stool, leaving her four-year-old daughter sitting on the floor and staring up at her in horror. Her daughter began to cry, and from then on, with every sighting of a spider, a ladybug, or an ant, her little girl became paralyzed by fear—fear that she had learned from her mother's own reactions. It was a rude awakening for this mom and she moved forward vowing to learn how to control her reactions to her fears; she even discovered that she learned her behaviors from her own mother.

As mothers, we are our children's first role models. And this truth is magnified when one is the mother of a daughter. Because they are the same sex, little girls look to their mothers as their first examples of womanhood—and even mimic their actions, responses, biases, beliefs, and mannerisms. Just as the young girl picked up cues from her mother regarding her fear of bugs, little girls look to their moms for evidence of the right way to live and behave. With this huge responsibility bestowed on mothers around the world, it's no wonder many of them are overwhelmed or sometimes confused by the daunting responsibility of raising girls in the twenty-first century.

Our culture's last major contribution to the psychology of girls, at least in the literary world, was Mary Pipher's *Reviving Ophelia*. While much in the world of adolescence has stayed the same since the initial publication of that book in 1994, much has also changed. Our little girls are facing big issues—you could even call them adult-size issues—and in most cases parents are not equipped to deal with them themselves, let alone be expected to help their daughters through them. That is why Erin Munroe wrote this book—to help parents help their daughters respond better—and why I am so excited about what it offers to parents on all issues, big or new or confusing.

Munroe, a licensed mental-health counselor, offers a parenting book that is as much for adolescent girls as it is for parents themselves. Like the woman in the above story who was afraid of bugs, many parents are so afraid or inexperienced with the many issues today's young girls face that they send the wrong messages to their daughters about how to deal with them. With no precedence to look back on or context or personal experiences to draw on, parents find it hard to understand what their daughters are experiencing, so they often project their own fears, misconceptions, and biases onto their daughters, causing further confusion and a cycle of fear and shame. According to Munroe, parents need to first control their reactions and step back to see the big picture to effectively guide their daughters through their big issue—and that is ultimately what makes this book so unique and effective.

When Big Issues Happen to Little Girls sheds light on the topics that little girls face today and how they have changed or evolved from times past. It also helps parents learn about themselves and their emotions so that they can better offer their daughters the coping mechanisms they need to become rational, independent thinkers who can confidently communicate with their parents and other caregivers and effectively respond to the demands of pressures they face today at younger and younger ages.

Let *When Big Issues Happen to Little Girls* become your twenty-first century parenting strategy and give your daughter the gift of resiliency and confidence that she is capable of experiencing and so deserving of receiving.

—**Michele Borba, Ed.D.**, *Today Show* contributor and
author of *The Big Book of Parenting Solutions:*
101 Answers to Your Everyday Challenges and Wildest Worries

PREFACE

When I was in graduate school, I never in a million years thought that I would end up working with children and adolescents—and loving it. Middle school was a horror show for me; memories of high school are still met with a wince and a sharp turn of my stomach. As part of my internship, I was forced to run a girl's group in a pretty tough middle school. The first few weeks were terrifying. They talked about bullying, poverty, abuse, fist fights, carrying weapons to school for protection, the adults they hated, the teachers who hated them, their fears, and of course how stupid they thought I was. I brought cookies; they wanted a different kind. I had markers; they wanted crayons. They asked intrusive questions about my life that I didn't want to answer. They challenged me by claiming I did not know what they were going through, nor would I ever have to live in their shoes. So what did I do? I bought different cookies; I borrowed crayons from the school secretary; I answered some of their questions; and I agreed with them—I did not know what they were going through. I would never walk in their shoes. But I would be there week after week, with my cookies,

my crayons, my nonjudgmental ears, and my desire to be someone
consistent, trustworthy, and compassionate in their lives.

It worked.

After a while (including a blizzard, two fist fights, and week where
they didn't show), they trusted that I would keep coming back. After
changing their cookie requests week after week, they knew that I
listened to them and that I was trying. They bounced things off me.
They considered some of my suggestions. They made fun of my
clothes, but told me I wouldn't be me without them. They pointed
out when my haircut looked hideous. I adored them. I may not have
known what it was like to be one of them, but I remembered how
tough it was to grow up. We found respect for one another and realized that we all had important things to say. It was an amazing, life-
changing experience. I was filled with empathy for these girls, and I
realized, this was right where I should be. My own angst still lived
on, but the memories that scarred me were memories that gave me
the ability to really hear these kids and respect their emotions.

When I graduated and moved into the workforce, I stuck to teenagers, and that quickly morphed into a job with children. I was and
still am intrigued by their thoughts, dreams, reactions, and emotions.
Kids are so funny. Behind the curtain of drama often lie nuggets of
genius. They look at the world in such a different, and often better,
way than we do. As much as we are trying to teach them, we could
stand to learn from them from time to time. Stop and listen. Don't
worry so much about what you are going to say; instead, listen to what
they really say and what they really need. Growing up is a process—
one that needs our support, love, and guidance. If we don't listen to
what they are asking us, and just assume we know what their needs
are, we will miss out on the opportunities they give us when they do
want to listen and are willing to hear our suggestions.

Listen to your little ones. Don't fill up too much space with your own voice. Be present for them. Shut off the cell phone. Turn off the television. Take the laptop out of the dining room. You won't have this opportunity again. Enjoy it.

INTRODUCTION

As a child and adolescent therapist, I am often in the position of having to tell the caring adults in my clients' lives that something major has occurred in their child's life. If I could change one thing about these meetings, it would be to take the caretakers outside and give them a quick session on how to best react to hearing this specific news. I'd give them a heads up that the news they're about to hear is tough, but that their initial reaction is going to impact their child forever, so please pull it together and fake a good reaction if necessary, and save the hyperventilating or swearing for later. Unfortunately, if I did that I would be letting the cat out of the bag, so I can only prep caretakers in general. As a therapist, I am trained to be rather stoic, even if the news is outrageous. As a parent, emotions run high, and even the calmest, most understanding parent can totally freak out when hearing troubling information.

This book will provide caretakers with the tools to offer the best reaction possible to some of the big issues girls may face. It will also discuss how to support girls as they deal with these issues, and how to promote healthy coping skills for girls so that they are less likely to turn to scary ways of coping.

In all honesty, the initial reaction adults have upon hearing about a child's involvement with troubling issues is likely to have a huge impact on what they tell us in the future. Should they trust us? Will they be afraid of how we might react? Will we be disappointed in them? Will we still love them? What will happen to them if we are mad at them? Will they be okay, and have us to protect them and keep them safe?

It is time to break open these big issues and deal with them in a healthy, supportive way so that girls will grow up to be well-adjusted young women.

ONE

Check Yourself Before You Wreck Yourself (and the Girl in Your Life!)

Adriana fidgeted in her chair as we both watched her mother pace back and forth behind the chairs. "Is there anyone else in the family who seems to be anxious like Adriana?"

Mom paused for a moment in her pacing, frowned at Adriana, and paced a bit faster. "No!" she announced, "I don't know where she gets it. It drives me insane. Why she can't just relax is beyond me." Mom continued her rambling as Adriana rolled her eyes and made a gesture that indicated that her mother was the cuckoo one.

Please try this exercise: Point at the most emotionally unstable, unpredictable, and dramatic person in the house—most likely, your daughter! Now, look at your hand. Notice how many fingers are pointing back at you. Hmmm. Interesting.

Take a moment to think. Could you be a little unstable, unpredictable, or dramatic? Do you handle everything perfectly all the time? If you do, good for you; you will have the healthiest kid around. If you don't, join the club and read on.

Surprisingly, our girls in all their craziness, angst, anger, anxiety, and drama take after us. They tend to act like the adults around them act; whether this is due to nature or nurture has yet to be discovered. How many adults do you know who are as cool as cucumbers these days? Not many, I would imagine.

How can we expect girls to handle everything well when we, the supposedly well-adjusted adults, so often handle things with stress, drama, impulsivity, and anger? What standards do you set for yourself? Are you a parent who is trying to work full time, bake the best brownies, take the right aerobics classes, have a floor clean enough to impress your mother-in-law, and all the while smiling and wearing the right pair of jeans (the pair that says I am cool without trying too hard)?

Whatever your role in your daughter's life, it is important that you recognize your own level of stress, anxiety, anger, and overall care for self. Living your life stressed out and forever trying to impress everyone teaches your daughter that you believe this is the way she should live. Even if you tell your daughter a million times that she shouldn't take on so much or that trying to impress everyone and doing too much at once is silly, what you are saying doesn't really matter if you are not setting a good example for her. The next time you reprimand her for her behavior, look closely at yourself and at the other adults in her life. Does anyone exhibit the kind of behavior for which she was reprimanded? Did she lash out at a friend before thinking about what she was going to say? Have you ever done this? Did she procrastinate before doing her homework? Does any adult in your household tend to procrastinate? Take notice of whether you are setting a not-so-fabulous example. It's not necessary to do everything flawlessly all the time, but be aware that when you behave in a way that you wouldn't want her to behave, it does have an impact on her. We all make mistakes. If you make a mistake, admit to it. This is better for your daughter than making excuses for yourself or denying that you have been engaging in behavior that sets a poor example.

How can you become a healthier role model for your daughter? Try to be as balanced as possible. Work on big things like self-care, stress reduction, and being true to oneself. Don't worry about little things like only eating three fruits or veggies a day instead of the recommended number, cleaning only what is visible, or hitting snooze an extra time (or two) on the weekends.

SELF-CARE

Do you devote enough attention to self-care? Having adult responsibilities makes "me time" very hard to come by, but even more important to find. Unless you take care of yourself, you will be shortchanging everyone who needs you. When you are well rested and well cared for, it is much easier and much more fun for you to take care of others. Instead of feeling put upon by always doing things for others and therefore getting annoyed by such things as the chatter between your daughter and her girlfriends when you are driving them from place to place, you might enjoy their chitchat and reminisce with them about your own teenage years.

In a study published in the *Journal of Health and Social Behavior,* researchers Ranae J. Evenson and Robin W. Simon found that "there is no type of parent that reports less depression than nonparents." With that in mind, self-care becomes even more important for parents than for nonparents, so get to it. Discussing this bit of research is not meant to scare you or encourage you to lock yourself in your bathroom, but instead to make you aware that parenting (biological, stepparenting, adoptive, or otherwise) puts you at risk for feeling depressed. So you really need to safeguard yourself against that risk as best you can. Self-care will help.

Another benefit of taking time for yourself is that by doing so, you are showing your daughter the importance of taking care of herself and modeling how to do so responsibly. For example, a ninety-minute bubble bath might be your way of relaxing and taking care of yourself. If you choose to take your relaxing bath at 6:00 AM on a Tuesday, however, when everyone in the house is trying to prep for work or school, you are likely to disrupt their schedules since they may need to use the bathroom to get ready for the day. Try to schedule your bath at a time that is not only convenient for you but also for everyone else in the household. Perhaps Sunday night might be a good night for a long bath because the kids will probably be working on their homework and your partner or another adult is likely to be available if they need help.

Explaining to your daughter that everyone will benefit from a bit of "me time" to check in with oneself and check out from everyone else can encourage her to take care of her needs now and in the future. You may find that you need to help her time it correctly or pick healthy ways of spending this time. Although diving into a huge ice cream sundae may sound like the ultimate reward, try to model healthy activities like going for a walk, taking quiet time in your room, drawing or painting, listening to music, working on a hobby, or reading. Make sure that she isn't ducking a family dinner every week or suddenly needing "me time" when she is supposed to be taking the dog for a walk.

Action 1: Schedule "me time" for yourself and announce it to those with whom you live. Post it on the fridge, write it on the calendar, or do whatever you need to do to set aside the time.

Make time for yourself. Can't find the time to do it? Then use half of your lunch break at work to listen to calming music or walk around the block. Talk about your "me time" when you get home so that other family members know that you are taking care of yourself. Encourage them to carve out some "me time" for themselves. They might all think that you are totally corny, and maybe you are, but if corniness is what you need to take care of yourself and to help those around you take care of themselves, then so be it.

STRESS REDUCTION

This goes hand in hand with self-care. One of the best ways to reduce stress is to take time for yourself, so you are already off to a great start! Girls are more stressed than ever these days, making it extremely important to show them how they can reduce the stress in their lives. A stressed out, frazzled caregiver who is trying to impress everyone and meet impossible deadlines is not the kind of role model your girl needs. But how can you reduce stress when you are trying to be so perfect?

- ☑ Stop trying to be perfect.
- ☑ You don't need to do it all.
- ☑ Make a to-do list for a typical day, if you don't already have one. It will probably look something like this:

Walk dogs, remind Adele to bring project to school, make doctor's appointment for self, make dentist appointment for Adele, make shot appointment for dogs, go to work, call friend who sucks the life out of you back while on lunch break, run wellness meetings at work, go to grocery store to buy ingredients for baked goods you promised for bake sale tomorrow, make dinner, help Adele with homework while cleaning the house (she can hear you over the vacuum, right?), make the baked goods with Adele, take the dogs and your partner for a walk, go to the weekly fund-raising meeting for Adele's school, try to squeeze in the gym, put Adele to bed.

Yikes! No wonder you are stressed out. But you have to do it all, right? Wrong! Prioritize. Do you need to call your life-sucking friend during lunch? No. Does it mean you are a bad friend? No, because you would have rolled your eyes the whole time she talked and resented her for filling your lunch hour with drivel. Do you have to run the wellness meeting at work? Well, your boss told you that if you did, you could have five comp days and that means an extra vacation week with the family in the summer. Okay, keep that one because the payoff rocks! Do the baked goods have to be home-made? No! Buy stuff at the grocery store bakery and don't volunteer to bake again. Do you have to walk the dogs or can your partner help you out? That one is debatable since exercise and time with your partner could be nice for your health and your relationship. Can you skip the fund-raising meeting and let them know that from now on, you will only be able to attend every other meeting?

Practice prioritizing. What can you cross off your to-do list forever? What can you delegate? What items will create stress now but have a payoff later? Is that payoff really worth the stress? Prioritizing and sticking to those tasks that are on your priority list will make you a better caregiver. It will show your daughter that you don't have to do it all. What are you trying to prove by doing so much, anyway? You will be wise to set a healthy example for your child.

Being overscheduled will only make you miserable anyway. Teach your daughter to avoid having too much on her plate by being comfortable saying "no." Committing to things that are high priorities and completing them well is more valuable than completing many things half-a**ed. The benefits for you and for your daughter will be great! You will have more time to spend doing things you really want to do together and spend less time running around in a state of stress doing things you consider burdensome.

Action 2: Prioritize your to-do list and get rid of unnecessary activities that add to your stress.

Stop trying to be perfect. Imagine if your parents were perfect. That would be pretty stressful for a child, don't you think? You don't have to be perfect, and in fact admitting that you aren't can take a load off your shoulders as well as your daughter's. If she knows that it is okay to make mistakes, she is going to feel a lot less pressure when she makes them. Knowing it is okay to make a mistake actually makes admitting you made a mistake a lot easier. So take it easy on yourself; it can only benefit your daughter.

Check your stress levels, keeping tabs on your stress just like you keep tabs on whether there is gas in your gas tank. Are you running on empty? Is stress sucking all the fuel out of you? Don't let yourself hit empty before you refuel. Do something that is stress-reducing when your tank is half full. You don't have to fill it all the way up, but do enough to bump it up to three-quarters of a tank.

Action 3: Come up with a list of stress-reducing activities you can do anywhere (such as deep breathing, taking a quick walk, meditating, or talking to a good friend). Practice at least one each week.

Be proactive about your health. Have you had your annual physical, dental cleanings, eye exam, and other preventative exams or screenings? Taking care of your health is extremely important. Many people don't go to the doctor until something is wrong; when times are tough, going to the dentist or eye doctor may seem like a luxury. If you stay ahead of health issues, however, you truly will be better off. A cavity that can be filled if you catch it early could become a root canal if you ignore it. Stay ahead of the game by making sure everything is up to date. This sets a great example for your children. It will help them learn to take their own health seriously. Also, if your doctor tells you to make changes in your life (healthier eating, more exercise, better sleep, and such), *do it!* Staying healthy will reduce your stress because you won't have to worry so much about the possibility of needing sick days, and you will feel better and more energetic.

Action 4: Schedule and attend preventative appointments. Make sure you know if you need a physical, eye exam, or dental appointment.*

BE TRUE

Be true to oneself. Really? Yes, really! If you can't be true to yourself, how do you expect your beautiful daughter to stick up for herself when the cool girl in class tells her that her favorite socks are ugly and make her look stupid? Are you doing what you love, or at least trying? By now money has most likely played a part in your job decisions, so if your dream was to be an actress and you never made it big, you are likely doing something else to pay the bills. But did you leave acting behind completely? Is there a part of you that secretly dreams about acting again? Then make moves to do so in some way. Can you start a holiday tradition where each family member is responsible for creating and acting out a skit? Can you squeeze in an acting class? Do you have time in your schedule to try out for the local theater?

A little disclaimer: Going to these appointments may raise your stress level, but you will be relieved that you went once you have gone!

Don't lose sight of your dreams even though you are a grown up. Your dreams may not have come true in the way you wanted them to, but that doesn't mean they cannot be realized in some fashion. Be creative and find a way to bring passion into your life. Share your passion with your daughter so she understands that dreaming and being passionate about something is important. Help her understand that passions are what keep us going.

Action 5: Share your dreams and activities you are passionate about with your daughter. Find a way to incorporate them into your life today.

You have five actions to take this week. They should be fun to do, not stressful. Being a role model does not mean being perfect and doing it all. Instead, it means admitting your faults, recovering from mistakes, improving on areas that you aren't so hot in, being open to learning from others, and cultivating your passions and dreams. Stop worrying about what everyone thinks of you and recognize the importance of being someone who is trying to raise a young woman who can truly take care of herself.

Chapter 1:
Action Recap

Action 1: Schedule "me-time" for yourself and announce it to those with whom you live. Post it on the fridge, write it on the calendar, or do whatever you need to do to set aside the time.

Action 2: Prioritize your to-do list and get rid of unnecessary activities that add to your stress.

Action 3: Come up with a list of stress-reducing activities you can do anywhere (such as deep breathing, taking a quick walk, meditating, or talking to a good friend). Practice at least one each week.

Action 4: Schedule and attend preventative appointments. Make sure you know if you need a physical, eye exam, or dental appointment.

Action 5: Share your dreams and activities you are passionate about with your daughter. Find a way to incorporate them into your life today.

Revisit this list from time to time and make sure you are being the healthiest role model possible.

Chapter 1:
Top Five Talking Points

1. I am going to start setting aside time each week to just do something I would like to do. Hopefully it will help me become less stressed so I can be a better parent.

2. My goal is to stress less, so I can care for you more and really be present when you need me.

3. I am going to start doing yoga (or whatever I choose to do) each week to help reduce my stress. Is there anything I might like to try? Is there anything I find stress relieving?

4. I hope you know I am also trying to set a good example for you so you don't grow up thinking it is normal to be stressed and frazzled all the time.

5. I want you to know how important it is to continue to take care of yourself and your health, so I have to stay on top of my doctor's appointments as much as I stay on top of yours.

TWO

Growing Up Girl

"One minute, she is telling me how depressed she is. The next minute, she is looking in the mirror talking about how pretty she is and how all the boys like her. Then I find out that she has been cutting herself. She is either totally crazy, or she is just doing all of this to get attention."

Well, she probably is depressed, she probably does have moments when she thinks she looks cute, she probably feels a self-esteem boost when she hears that boys like her, and she probably really, really, really, above all else, needs your attention. Why is she all over the place? She is growing up girl.

Parents often come in at their wit's end about girls who are between the ages of nine and fourteen. All of a sudden, their sweet girls have become moody, oppositional, unpredictable, and uninterested in the activities they once loved. Common statements include:

"What does go on in that head of hers? She is *crazy!!!*"

"Can you test her to see if there is some sort of chemical imbalance? There must be."

"I don't know what to do with her. She wants more responsibility one day, and then she tells me she is overwhelmed the next day."

"She hates me, she hates her father, and she hates her little sister. Then she cries when her little sister doesn't want to talk to her. I don't know what her deal is!!"

"She used to love going to the art museum with me, and painting on her own. I was in her room the other day and all her paints were thrown in a box in the back of her closet. The closest thing she has to paint now is her nail polish!"

Well, she isn't crazy, but between peer pressure, hormones, and brain development, she probably feels pretty crazy, and you might think she acts crazy more often than not. As if the developing brain wasn't enough, her hormones are surging, and social pressures are at their highest. Peer pressure and puberty get their own chapters. This chapter is all about the brain, and really a girl's brain could have its own book. The brain is absolutely amazing and at the same time very overwhelming. You don't need to understand too much about the brain to appreciate what is going on in your daughter's brain. The best way I have ever heard it explained was by Elizabeth Driscoll Jorgensen, CADC, Insight Counseling, in Ridgefield, Connecticut:

"Their brains are all limbic right now. We as parents need to be their prefrontal cortex, and we can't take their limbic systems personally."

This quote, once you have a better understanding of the brain, will sum up your daughter's brain perfectly!

THE ANATOMY OF THE BRAIN

There is white matter, gray matter, the amygdala, the corpus callosum, neurons, synapses, the limbic system, the prefrontal cortex, and more. Do you need to know about all of these areas to understand your daughter's brain and how it is developing? No. What you do need to appreciate is that her brain is not fully developed, and the parts that aren't developed are the parts we all wish would just hurry up and develop. The two parts of the brain we are going to focus on are the limbic system and the prefrontal cortex. And by focus on, this is really just a quick-and-dirty description of these two parts of the brain.

The limbic system is the emotional part of the brain. It is the part that is responsible for behavior, emotions, motivation, laughter, pleasure, the survival instinct, and more. This is the part of the brain that drives your daughter at this time. She is basically thinking and acting with the help of this emotional mind. So when she seems extra emotional, she is. She truly is experiencing her life as a crazy roller coaster of emotions. When she tells you her life is over because the boy of her dreams saw the zit on her forehead, she *feels* that her life as she knows it is over in many ways because he saw this zit on her head. Now you, with all of your experience, developed brain, and regulated hormones, are probably thinking, "Oh great, here she goes again. She will probably hate that boy next week, and forget she even had the zit." True! This is why she needs you. Not to invalidate her by telling her that she is being ridiculous, but by hearing her out and letting her know that even though it may feel like the end of the world, she really will be okay. The zit will go away, and life will go on. So when you look at your daughter, think limbic system—emotions, instinct, motivation.

The next part of the brain you need to know about is the prefrontal cortex. It was once believed that the prefrontal cortex finished developing in adolescence, but more recent research has shown that it actually isn't fully developed until we are in our twenties. The prefrontal cortex is the part of the brain that is often considered the "executive functioning" of our brains. Tasks like planning, organizing, and decision making are taken care of in the prefrontal cortex. Since it hasn't fully developed, our girls might not be as capable as we think they are of making good decisions. It is almost like the filter for their emotions isn't quite fine-tuned enough yet. So when they react to something, they react with great emotion, and without the restraint, and decision making that develops in time and through experience.

So now that you understand what these two parts of the brain do, let's go back to the quote from Elizabeth Driscoll Jorgensen, but replace a few words:

"Their brains are all emotions right now. We as parents need to be their decision making, and we can't take their emotional behaviors personally."

How does that sound? So when you look at your daughter and think, *she must be bananas. She makes the worst decisions ever and she is an emotional wreck,* just think how lucky she is to have you!! You are right! She is an emotional wreck (limbic system, hormones, friends who are also hormonal), and she needs help with making decisions. That is why you are there. You really do need to make some decisions for her.

Despite the fact that there are parts of your daughter's brain that haven't finished developing, this isn't a blanket excuse for all of her behaviors. This is something for you as the parent to remember when she is really driving you nutty, acting crazily emotional, and taking you on a roller coaster ride. This is meant to help you put some of your daughter's actions into perspective, but you don't want to use it as an excuse for all of her defiant behaviors or her repeated poor decisions. She is capable of learning better decision making, planning, and organization. So when she breaks curfew for the third time and tells you, "Oh, it was my darn limbic system again!" that is not the case. She is not incapable of doing the right thing; she just needs help finding her way.

Another note of advice that Elizabeth Driscoll Jorgensen gives to many parents is, "Don't go limbic on limbic. You will not win." As they say, don't fight fire with fire. When your daughter is getting emotional with you, if you fight back as an emotional mess yourself, the two of you are just going to end up emotionally drained and exhausted. Take a moment, tap into that prefrontal cortex that you have developed, and show some restraint. Be reasonable, calm, direct, and kind with your daughter.

Action 1: Appreciate that your daughter's brain is going through changes and that her prefrontal cortex has yet to completely develop.

What other changes are girls facing between the ages of eight and fourteen? In an interview with Harriette Wimms, Ph.D., from the Mariposa Child Success Programs in Towson, Maryland, Dr. Wimms reminds parents that girls are going through a number of cognitive, emotional, behavioral, and psychosocial changes between the ages of eight and fourteen. They are moving away from learning through play to learning through formal education. Likewise, changes in cognition bring about changes in emotions and how they are expressed. Interactions with peers and adults shape their behavior, perceptions, and beliefs. These are major changes in developmental processes for girls—changes that require parents' awareness, understanding, and patience. It is also the time that children move from prepubescence through puberty. The hormones that rage during this time in a girl's body are unpredictable to her. She doesn't know when or why she will be feeling what. These changes also require mental shifts. Depending on her age and school district, she is moving from elementary school to middle school, and then to high school. Tangible and intangible transitions make up her world. Some are expected, and some come by surprise. All of these changes can be overwhelming to her.

Dr. Wimms reports that in the child success programs at Mariposa, they are careful to have empathy for what the parents find stressful. The little girl who has always held a parent's hand proudly is now walking ahead of the parent at the mall. The little girl who loved having a parent brush her hair now wants to dye it purple. The fear that you are somehow losing her is so real for you. You need to respect your feelings in all of this, and appreciate that your feelings are sometimes going to cloud your own judgment. So, as much as you respect her emotions, give yourself time and space to respect your own.

Action 2: Appreciate the changes that are going on for her, how they affect her, and also how they affect you.

How can you help with the changing brain, the raging hormones, and the excessive emotions? Well, you can't control them; you are going to have to roll with them. When your daughter is angry, sad, cranky, or gloomy, and you want to know why, stop yourself. She might not know. She might know, but if she says, "I don't know," she really might not. You may have to help her figure out what it is that is making her so cranky. You might even need to point out to her that she is cranky. Here is an example:

"Glenny, you seem like you are cranky today. Is something going on? Were there any stressful or frustrating things that went on today?"

Glenny rolls her eyes and raises her voice as she speaks, "I don't know! Nothing is going on. I am not cranky!"

"Okay. You just seemed cranky, that's all. I wanted to make sure you knew you could talk to me if there was something that was making you unhappy. Sometimes, sweetie, you might just feel cranky for no reason, and that's okay, too."

Anne Townsend, Ph.D., from Mariposa Child Success Programs, suggests that parents validate the emotions their daughters are feeling, and then help them shift out of them. We stuff their feelings too often by stopping them, and forcing them to move on from them before they are ready. You need to be able to stay in the emotional state with her before helping her move on. This can be tough; it can be time-consuming. When your daughter is crying over the boy who ignores her, and you need to get your other daughter to lacrosse, get dinner on the table, pick your mother up from yoga, walk the dog, handle paperwork, and pay bills, it is really hard to stop and sit with her while she feels terrible—for the second time this week. It is especially tough when you know she will probably be fine tomorrow, and when she tends to be a bit overly dramatic. But stop. Dinner can wait; you can be five minutes late picking up your mother; and the dog will survive.

Look at the difference between these approaches. Instead of saying, "Oh, Marie, you will be fine! Come on now, focus on your homework," sit down, put your hand on hers, and say something more empathic. "Oh, Marie. It sounds like you feel awful. I am so sorry. It really stinks to feel this way." Sit with her and listen to her. It probably won't take as long as you think it will take. Then you can say, "I am going to run some errands. Do you feel okay to stay here and do your homework, or do you want to come with me and do your homework when we get home?"

Action 3: Validate her feelings and help her shift from those feelings when the time is right.

Why is it so important to support this social emotional development? Shouldn't we focus more on our daughter's academics? Dr. Townsend notes that children with better social emotional skills are better off academically in the long run. When kids become stressed, there is a physiological response. Kids with better social emotional skills are able to rebound faster from the physiological response their bodies have from stress. This is protective for them because kids who stay in that physiological stress response for prolonged periods of time are more likely to become depressed. Depression and anxiety hinder performance in important places like school and sports.

Action 4: Support her social emotional development for short- and long-term benefits.

What should our expectations be? With all these changes going on, are we expecting too much? There is the changing brain and body, the stress of growing up, hormones, which interfere physiologically, and then the stress of expectations that are beyond their capabilities. So how do we come up with appropriate expectations? Do we need to tiptoe around them? No. Should we tell them to suck it up? No. We can encourage our daughters to do their best, but support them by checking in frequently. Is your daughter overwhelmed? Did she do what you expected? If not, why? Is there a skill she is lacking? If so, can you teach her that skill? Figuring out what you can expect from your daughter is often a guessing game, but if you put expectations on her that are open for discussion, or that lead to teachable moments, she shouldn't feel overwhelmed. This is a new venture for you as much as it is for her. You can have expectations, but if she isn't quite where you think she should be, have patience. Teach her the skills you think she needs.

Action 5: Work to set realistic expectations. Instead of feeling disappointment if she doesn't meet them, seize the teachable moment.

What is to blame for this difficult road for our daughters— hormones, brain development, society, or all of the above? According to both Dr. Wimms and Dr. Townsend, changes in hormones significantly impact cognitive functioning and mood management. This directly impacts their social interactions. The development of emotion regulation and executive functioning are also interrelated. They both affect learning and social skills. When you are stressed you produce cortisol, which impairs working memory. Helping your daughter regulate her mood, decrease stress, and learn executive-functioning skills will help make life a bit less stressful. Not only can you directly teach many of the skills your daughter needs right now, but also you can model appropriate behaviors, planning, social interactions, and more. She can learn so much that can make her road a bit smoother.

Action 6: Model appropriate behaviors, help her keep her stress level down, and help her regulate her moods.

Chapter 2:
Action Recap

Action 1: Appreciate that your daughter's brain is going through changes and that her prefrontal cortex has yet to completely develop.

Action 2: Appreciate the changes going on for her, how they affect her, and also how they affect you.

Action 3: Validate her feelings and help her shift from those feelings when the time is right.

Action 4: Support her social emotional development for short- and long-term benefits.

Action 5: Work to set realistic expectations. Instead of feeling disappointment if she doesn't meet them, seize the teachable moment.

Action 6: Model appropriate behaviors, help her keep her stress level down, and help her regulate her moods.

Chapter 2:
Top Five Talking Points

SHUSH

Here is an easy acronym to remind you of how to react to your daughter when she is freaking out or if there is a big issue:

S: **Shush!** Shut your mouth and be quiet.

H: **Hear.** Listen to your daughter and actually hear what she is trying to tell you.

U: **Understand.** Try to put yourself in her shoes for a moment so you can better understand what she is going through and have empathy.

S: **Support.** Let her know that you are there to support her through this tough time and get her the help she needs.

H: **Hug.** Hug her tight. Let her know that you love her.

THREE

Frenemies

Olivia has always been friends with Danya. Olivia's mother noticed that Danya wasn't around as much anymore, and she was really surprised when Olivia didn't invite Danya to her birthday dinner. Olivia's mom didn't know what to do. She knew Danya's mother pretty well from school activities, but she wasn't sure if calling her would embarrass Olivia. Olivia's mom decided to talk with Olivia about Danya. Olivia seemed very frustrated by the conversation. She told her mom, "Danya and I just don't hang out anymore. No big deal."

Olivia's mom continued to question her, "Who is Danya hanging out with then? It seems like you and the rest of the girls are still friendly. I always liked Danya. She seems like a very polite and sweet girl."

Olivia looked guilty and sighed, "Danya is nice, Mom. She just isn't really that cool to hang out with anymore. I guess we are just going our separate ways."

Olivia's mom was stumped. Since when did it matter if someone was cool or not? She thought she had taught Olivia to like people for who they are and to not get pulled into popularity contests. "I hope you aren't being mean to Danya. I hope this is a mutual decision to give your friendship a rest." Olivia looked uncomfortable and went up to do her homework. Olivia's mom remained concerned, but she hoped they would work it out.

A few weeks went by. Olivia's birthday dinner came and went, and there was still no talk of Danya. These days, kids have their own cell phones, or they keep their conversations to texting, Facebooking, instant messaging (IM), or other fairly private ways of connecting. Because of this, Olivia's mom didn't know that Danya was calling and trying to reach out to Olivia. Olivia had unfriended her on Facebook, blocked her from AIM, and simply ignored her phone calls and texts. In times when everyone had to use the home phone, Olivia's mom would have picked up rather quickly on the fact that Olivia was purposely avoiding Danya. Luckily for everyone, Danya's mom caught on to what was happening and called Olivia's mom.

Come to find out, Olivia and the rest of the girls Danya had been friendly with had ousted Danya, claiming she cared too much about her grades, she was a baby, she was a wannabe, no one liked her, her clothes weren't right, her hair looked stupid, and so on. And Danya heard these nasty things twenty-four hours a day. The girls texted mean messages, posted embarrassing moments of Danya's on Facebook, talked about her at lunch, and told everyone else in school to block Danya from their IMing because she was a loser and no one should associate with a loser. Danya's mom told Olivia's mom that Danya had become really depressed since this started and she wasn't coming out of her room much. She was refusing to go to school or to other activities, claiming that she was sick. Danya's mom said she took Danya's phone away one night and it buzzed with nasty text messages all night long.

Olivia's mom was horrified and heartbroken. How could her daughter do something so cruel? Danya's mom said that Olivia never sent negative messages and didn't have anything cruel on her Facebook about Danya, so that is why she called Olivia's mom first—in the hope that reaching out to Olivia might be a safe start. Although Olivia's mom was glad to hear that Olivia wasn't being as cruel as the others, she told Danya's mother that she felt Olivia was just as hurtful and at fault for not sticking up for Danya and for following the other girls in blocking her and ignoring her. Olivia's mom agreed to meet with Danya's mom and the school counselor to figure out how to best take care of the situation.

Think this situation is outrageous? It happens every day and you can pretty much count on your daughter being involved in a situation like this either as the bully, the bullied, or the standby. Girls learn to be competitors early on, and cliques and bullying are present earlier than ever before. One day your daughter is in, the next day your daughter is shunned by the whole school. Think your girls are safe until high school? Junior high? Try elementary school. Not only are girls subject to bullying and cliques, but also the extent to which bullying can take place is growing ever larger than life. Technological advancements in bullying have made the game quite unfair.

As parents, it is really tricky to keep tabs on our kids and make sure they are being nice members of society. It was much easier years ago!! Think about it. Before, the home phone was the only means of communication and more kids went home after school to a supervised setting. These days, kids can communicate by cell (talking or texting) and computers (e-mail, Facebook, instant messaging, and more). With more parents working full time, many kids go home to an unsupervised house. It is no wonder bullying has become such a terrible and frightening issue! There is no escape from a bully. A bully can get to you directly or indirectly all day and all night long. Should adults step in? If so, how should they go about it? Let's look at the scenario from above, and address each role—the bully, the standby, and the bullied—separately.

THE BULLY

The bully in this story is a very popular girl, Krista, who had begun to dislike Danya. Danya was closer to Olivia, teachers liked Danya, parents liked Danya, and boys liked Danya, so basically Krista didn't like that everyone liked Danya. In Krista's eyes, Danya was stealing Krista's thunder, while all Danya was doing was being herself. What Krista did to Danya was horrible. So why are we even talking about her? Poor Danya; she is the one we should discuss. While that is true, everyone involved played a role; to not address the bully and her behavior would be to ignore a key player in the drama. If we don't take a close look at her actions and the reasoning behind them, we won't really solve the problem. Krista will be likely to do it again. Although many parents and other caretakers will hate to even consider this, your daughter could be the bully, not the bullied. It is important to know what to watch for in case your daughter is bullying others.

Action 1: Recognize if your daughter is developing any bullying behaviors by observing and talking to other adults in the community (such as coaches or teachers).

The goal should be to have a daughter who does not bully anyone! First of all, teach her from the start to be nice to and respect others. Second of all, catch a negative attitude early. If your daughter is mean to kids on the playground when she doesn't get her way or when she wants something someone else has, nip it in the bud. Don't tolerate that sort of behavior. If you find she still behaves badly, talk to a counselor about different discipline strategies or even about group counseling. Group counseling is often very effective since members are called out on negative behaviors by their peers. Feedback is often more meaningful to kids when it comes from a peer instead of a parent. Third, and perhaps most important, do you make fun of others? Do you tease your daughter relentlessly about sensitive subjects? Does your partner? Is there another family member who bullies your daughter or somehow teaches her that being mean to others is a great way to make her feel better about herself? If you are doing any of these things—Stop. If someone else is doing these sorts of things, don't let him or her get away with it! Letting someone else bully your daughter because it doesn't seem that bad, or it is just her older sister, (that's what sisters do), is not okay. You are telling everyone that it is okay with you if bullying goes on, and setting a poor example for your daughter.

Action 2: Check in on where she might be learning this behavior. If it is in your household, take action immediately and do not tolerate it.

Could your daughter already be bullying? How is she with her friends? Do they change often? Have you seen her tease friends in a way that is not well-received by her friends? Have parents called you or commented that your daughter is mean to others or not fitting in well? Has the school called you with concerns? When you check her cell phone and computer (more on that below!), does she post negative comments about others? Is she secretive about what she is doing online and on her phone? If any of these ring true and you are concerned, start investigating on your own by talking to people involved with your daughter outside of the home—other parents, coaches, school personnel, relatives, and others. It is really important that you take responsibility for your daughter and her behavior before it gets out of hand.

She is a bully. And you know it. What can you do? Get support for yourself. Talk to others, such as your family, primary care physician, school personnel, or a counselor, to get ideas on how to remedy the situation. Make sure they know you want to address the problem and that you will not tolerate your daughter's behavior. No one wants his or her child to be bullied, but having a bully as your child can be quite tough, too. You aren't going to get much sympathy from others, and you are going to have to deal with many angry parents who are upset with you. Our kids are like our "mini-mes." People just assume that they act as we do. If they misbehave, people label their parents as poor disciplinarians, neglectful, or poor role models.

Do take a look at your household and make sure that these things are not true. Commit to spending more time with your child if need be to watch what she is doing and work with her on her behaviors. Find a counselor or a mentor with whom she can talk. Make sure that she understands that you are in contact with school employees, other parents, and people in the community. If you learn of any bullying behaviors, there will be consequences.

Action 3: Reach out for help and let others, including your daughter, know that you will not tolerate bullying behaviors.

Let her know that you love her and want to get to the root of the problem. You are angry, ashamed, frustrated, disappointed, and more, but you want to find out what is going on with her. If her friends have turned on her due to her bullying ways, she might feel very depressed and not know how to go about mending relationships. You will need to be there for her while also monitoring her behaviors and teaching her how to change her negative behaviors to positive ones.

On the other hand, she might be experiencing a jump in her social status because of her bullying ways. If this is so, you will have a harder time getting her to stop bullying. If she is experiencing any type of social gain for her negative behaviors, she might not really care what you think. In this case, you will need the school to be as firm as you are in dismantling any positive reinforcement she might be getting from peers for negative behaviors.

Action 4: Love your daughter by getting her the help she needs, remaining consistent in disciplining negative behaviors, and encouraging positive behaviors.

THE STANDBY

A standby is trickier to spot, and even trickier to change. She doesn't actively engage in bullying, but she also doesn't actively stick up for the person being bullied. So what should you do with her? If she isn't directly involved, she might not have much impact on the bully. Sticking up for the victim, however, might make the victim feel less alone. If she is directly in the circle of friends who is bullying someone, her voice will matter even more. She will have an impact if she joins in with the bullying or if she stands up for the person being bullied. It is really hard to be the one that sticks up for someone when it is her own friends who are being mean. It is much easier to join in or to try and fade into the background. Chuckling with the bully when she makes a nasty remark may seem harmless, but in fact it is extremely harmful. It is the standbys that the bullied person will look to for help, or hope. It is the standbys that the bullies look to for support as well. The people the bully is trying to get on her side are the ones that the bullied feels desperate to have stick up for her. Think of the standby as the swing vote. On a day when someone is being teased or harassed, a standby can make all the difference in the world even if all she does is say, "Hey cut it out." She doesn't need to fight the fight for anyone, but she has tremendous power in letting everyone know that she thinks what is going on needs to stop.

Could she do more than that? Absolutely. She could talk to the friend who is being mean and tell her that she is not going to hang around with her anymore until she knocks it off. She can reach out to the girl who is being bullied and tell her that the bully is being unfair and cruel. She could also talk to adults and make them aware of the situation so they can step in.

How can you tell if your daughter is a standby? It is tough. You really have to get to know your daughter, her friends, and how your daughter reacts in social situations. Observing her in social situations is the best way to figure it out, but you might not see many of the social situations in which she is involved since they tend to occur out of the home. Ask teachers and coaches how your daughter is in tough situations; they are more likely to have witnessed situations where your daughter had an opportunity to stick up for someone.

Action 1: Try and figure out if your daughter is a standby.

Regardless of whether you conclude that your daughter is a standby or not one, educating your daughter on how to effectively and safely stick up for other people is a nice idea. Safety is very important. You should make sure that your daughter can read the temperature of a situation. Is the situation heated? Is the bully threatening people with physical harm? Is bullying occurring in a space where adults are out of reach? Are there potential weapons? If the situation is too hot, get out and get help. Does this sound ridiculous to you? Is the idea of kids bringing weapons into a playground a foreign one? It happens more often than you might think. Both you and your daughter need to understand that her safety comes first. She won't be able to stick up for or help anyone if she is injured or compromised. If the situation could be dangerous, your daughter needs to know how to summon help. If she has a cell phone, make sure that she has local emergency numbers plugged in as well as emergency contact numbers for you and other adults who are trustworthy. Let her know that she will not get into trouble with you if she calls for help, and promise to help her if she finds herself in this sort of situation.

Action 2: Make sure that your daughter knows how to tell if a situation is potentially dangerous, and what to do in that type of situation.

If the bullying is occurring in a supervised place like in a school, at a sport practice, on the Internet, or by phone, teach her how to stick up for someone. She can do something as low-key as telling the bully to "Knock it off." She could also pull the person who is being bullied aside and say, "Just ignore her; she isn't being very nice." She could ramp it up a notch and state, "If you don't knock it off, I am going to get the principal." One of the best ways to teach your daughter how to handle these sorts of situations is by role-playing, or by watching movies or television shows that have scenes involving bullies. If you watch an episode of a show where someone simply stands by, ask your daughter what she would have done differently. Ask her what she would have wanted the standby to do to help if she were the one being bullied. This can generate a great discussion and also teach your daughter some cool ways of sticking up for others.

When it comes to the Internet and texting, she can simply show you what is going on, and you can take care of it on an adult level by calling the school counselor or other parents involved. You are usually better off calling a neutral party so that it won't be obvious that it was your daughter who brought attention to the issue. A school counselor or administrator can address the problem without revealing that your daughter was the one who called attention to the problem.

Action 3: Teach your daughter how to stick up for someone by role-playing, watching movies or television depicting situations involving bullies, and by role-modeling.

THE BULLIED

This is every parent's nightmare. No one wants his or her child to be the victim of bullying. When a child is the victim of bullying, primal instincts tend to take over. The parent of the child who is being bullied often wants to give mean kids and their parents a piece of his or her mind. If you do this, it is important that you do it calmly and in a way that makes the situation better, not worse. How do you know if your daughter is the victim of bullying? Keep tabs on her Internet and cell phone use (there is a section on this at the end of this chapter!), talk to her about how things are going with her friends, and observe how she interacts with them. Does she let them push her around? Does she seem anxious when she is around them? Get to know the parents of her friends; make sure you bring up any concerns about what you notice going on between the girls. Check in with your daughter and be aware of any changes in her mood, appetite, irritability, or hygiene, or in the amount of time she spends on the computer or cell phone—or with friends. Ask her straight out if people are being mean to her. If you discover that she is being bullied, let her know that you are going to do something to stop it. She may protest to save face, out of fear that this will only make the situation worse. You must take action anyway. You are the adult and you do know best. Yes, having you involved could temporarily make things even more uncomfortable for her. But in the long run, people will come to know that you are a parent who will get involved if something bad is happening. Your daughter will have the comfort of knowing that you will stick up for her and get the message that bullying is not okay. If you are concerned about getting involved because she seems so horrified, don't be. If this is occurring, her social life has already been disrupted.

Action 1. Take action and don't let it continue.

How can you become involved without causing further damage? Talking to school administrators is often a good place to start. If the bullying is going on at school, talking to school personnel can often be quite helpful. If they know about it, they can sometimes mediate a parent meeting, help curtail the bullying in school, punish negative behaviors, and support your daughter by doing such things as changing her classes, making sure she is not alone, and providing a safe place for her to go on a bad day. Make sure the school is doing everything they can do. If the majority of bullying is taking place there, they need to take action immediately.

If the bullying is taking place primarily outside of school, talking to the parents of the other girls involved is necessary. Before speaking to them, decide on an approach. Are you at the point that you will seek legal advice on how to go about pressing charges? Do you simply want to try and talk it out with the parent first? If the parent is not receptive, will you let her know that you will pursue other venues such as pressing charges? Figure out what you plan to say before you say it. It may even help to write down what you plan to say, as it will probably help you to organize your thoughts. This is about your child. Don't be surprised if you get emotional. Writing down what you want to say will help you to stay on point. Before ending the conversation, make sure there is a resolution. For example, a possible resolution might be that the other parent agrees to punish her child and if it happens again, you and the other parent will have a plan for the next course of action to resolve the matter (i.e., you will pursue legal measures, or you will involve the school if you haven't already).

Action 2: Speak to school personnel, coaches, parents, and other adults who may be involved or who may have witnessed the bullying. Make sure that they are doing everything they can for your daughter.

Now that you are taking action against the people who are bullying your daughter, it is important that you find someone in whom she can confide. Maybe she already has someone she feels comfortable talking to; if so, that is great. If she doesn't, find someone in whom she can confide and garner support. You can be there for her as well. However, she needs to have access to someone who is removed from the situation and can help her work on dealing with the day-to-day stress, building her self-esteem, and doing everything she can to keep this from happening to her and to others. Make sure the person your daughter speaks to can monitor her mood and check for warning signs of suicidality or increasing depression.

Action 3: Get your daughter help outside of the home.

The bully may respond immediately to interventions, and end all nastiness right away. Don't be surprised, however, if the bullying resurfaces. Your daughter also may report that the bullying has ended, but you may later find that it is continuing—although it may be carried out in a way that is more hidden. You must maintain a dialogue with your daughter about this to make sure it isn't resurfacing or getting worse. Your daughter may be reluctant to reveal what is going on. You really do need to know what is happening and she needs to know that you will remain involved until the situation is truly over.

Your daughter might be more than annoyed by you; she might be pissed! Continue to tell her that you love her and that your job is to keep her safe and happy. Do try to be as bearable as possible. Watch your own behavior; don't walk around screaming at people or demanding that people take care of things. Stay calm (even if you are burning up inside), and handle yourself with dignity. If the issue does not resolve, seek legal advice and let someone do the talking for you.

Listen to your daughter; really listen to what she has to say. Does she want to switch schools? Does she want a ride to school instead of taking the bus for a while? Would she feel better if she could switch her math class? You don't want her quitting everything in her life because of the bully, but you do want her to feel safe. If going to a new school will help her to feel safe, it is something you should consider.

Action 4: Continue to have a dialogue about bullying and social difficulties, while reminding her that you are there for her, you hear her, and you love her.

SCHOOL RESPONSIBILITY

Schools are taking on a lot of responsibility for handling situations involving bullying. This is understandable since a lot of bullying occurs at school. Schools also are one of the few places where adults have the opportunity to observe bullying firsthand and intervene. The unfortunate piece of this is that schools are sometimes held responsible for not doing enough about bullying situations, when schools are only part of the equation. Parents need to be more involved and take action themselves. The school can certainly be of great assistance or of no assistance. It is important to feel that your daughter's school is keeping her as safe as possible from bullying. If you don't think the school is doing enough, ask to see their bullying policy. Do they even have one? If so, are they following it? Is it a fair policy? Become familiar with your school's policy before you have to and see how you feel about it. Discuss any concerns you have with school administrators. PTO or school committee meetings might provide an opportunity to raise any concerns.

Become familiar with your daughter's school staff. Get to know the school secretary, school nurse, and cafeteria staff. These folks often know more about what goes on in a school than anyone else. Kids confide in the school secretaries all the time. Kids also chat up the nurse, and the nurse always knows the patterns of when kids are "sick." The cafeteria is a key place in the social structure of any school. The cafeteria staff knows where kids usually sit, with whom they sit, and if any dynamics change. Don't expect the school to solve the bullying issue for you, but do expect them to partner with you in refusing to tolerate bullying.

Action 1: Get to know the school's bullying policy and key people in the school.

In an article from the October 2009 *Journal of Adolescent Health,* it was found that rates of having bullied others or having been bullied at school at least once in the last two months were 20.8 percent physically, 53.6 percent verbally, 51.4 percent socially, or 13.6 percent electronically. One protective factor associated with less involvement in all types of bullying was higher parental support. So get involved with your daughter; know what is going on in her life!

KNOW YOUR DAUGHTER "IN"TERNET AND OUT!

As mentioned earlier, supporting your daughter and knowing what is going on in her life are very important. Make sure you know who her friends are and ask questions about her friendships frequently. Ask questions about her day, such as:

●

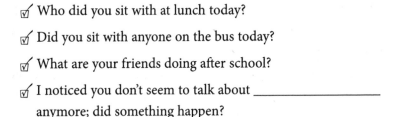

☑ Who did you sit with at lunch today?

☑ Did you sit with anyone on the bus today?

☑ What are your friends doing after school?

☑ I noticed you don't seem to talk about _____ anymore; did something happen?

Don't let your daughter mumble "Fine" to the "How was your day?" question and move on. Find out how she is really doing and be attuned to any changes in her friends.

Action 1: Know your daughter's social scene and ask questions about it to stay informed.

Find out what she does on her cell phone. Is she a texter? Check her phone to find out if she texts and the general gist of her texting. Do you have to read her texts all the time? No. But check in randomly. She deserves privacy, so you have to respect her needs. However, if you notice that she is particularly upset after texting, find out what is going on.

Action 2: Keep tabs on the cell phone.

Cyberspace can be really confusing. There are a bunch of different ways to communicate on the computer—MySpace, IMing, AIM, Facebook, blogging, webpages, and e-mail, to name a few. If your daughter has any social media pages, you need to be her friend on these, or have access by asking her for her password. Consider if she is mature enough to have access to these websites. There are plenty of kid-friendly sites she could peruse that are designed to keep kids safe from bullying. Cyberbullying and other Internet concerns have become so common that many states offer Internet safety programs for children and their guardians. It is worth it to take one if there is one offered in your town.

Here are two examples of what can happen in cyberspace:

Franny the Facebooker: Franny was a fun-loving fifth grader who didn't know much about the Internet. One day in school, a couple of girls were giggling at her. One walked by and commented "Nice Facebook status." Franny was confused, but didn't think anything of it. By the end of the day, however, other kids were teasing Franny about her status, calling her "thumb sucker" and "mama's baby." Upset, Franny went home and told her mom. Franny's mom happened to have a Facebook page of her own and searched for her daughter's name. Sure enough, there was a Facebook page under Franny's name, and the status update stated, "Sucking my thumb and cuddling with my Mama." Franny's mom was savvy enough to contact the folks at Facebook and have the page taken off since it was not Franny's doing. Mom also contacted the school and let them know what was going on. As fun as social media can be, it is scary that someone can basically pretend to be you and destroy your social life.

Another possible scenario involves instant messaging. In this instance, Jinny was IMing her friend Tasha, when suddenly Tasha started to say mean things to Jinny, "I actually hate you and think you are a b****." "No one likes you and John is cheating on you." Jinny was really surprised because this didn't sound like Tasha at all. Jinny ended up calling Tasha to yell at her for being so mean, only to find out that Tasha wasn't even on her computer. Another girl at school had gotten Tasha's information and logged in as Tasha, hoping to stir up trouble between Tasha and Jinny.

Craziness!!

If computers freak you out, find someone who can help you navigate them. An older niece or nephew might be able to help you. Your daughter's school also may have suggestions on how to make sure your daughter is using her computer in a way that is safe for her.

Action 3: Become Internet savvy.

Bullying has happened for years and it will continue to happen. The best you can do as a parent is get to know your child, her peer group, her school, her social habits, her Internet habits, and to be sensitive to any changes to her typical patterns. Bullying almost sounds like too kind a word to describe something that can be incredibly hurtful and damaging. Children have committed suicide because of the bullying they endured. It is a very serious problem that adults need to be aware of and ready to face. Awareness is definitely increasing, but it needs to build even more. There should be no-tolerance policies for bullying everywhere. You can start in your home with your children and make sure that they know that bullying will not be tolerated.

Chapter 3:
Action Recap

Bully Actions

Action 1: Recognize if your daughter is developing any bullying behaviors by observing and talking to other adults in the community (such as coaches or teachers).

Action 2: Check in on where she might be learning this behavior. If it is in your household, take action immediately and do not tolerate it.

Action 3: Reach out for help and let others, including your daughter, know that you will not tolerate bullying behaviors.

Action 4: Love your daughter by getting her the help she needs, remaining consistent in disciplining negative behaviors, and encouraging positive behaviors.

Standby Actions

Action 1: Try to figure out if your daughter is a standby.

Action 2: Make sure your daughter knows how to tell if a situation is potentially dangerous, and what to do in that type of situation.

Action 3: Teach your daughter how to stick up for someone by role-playing, watching movies or television depicting situations involving bullies, and by role-modeling.

Bullied Actions

Action 1: Take action and don't let it continue.

Action 2: Speak to school personnel, coaches, parents, and other adults who may be involved in the situation or witnessing the bullying. Make sure they are doing everything they can for your daughter.

Action 3: Get your daughter help outside of the home.

Action 4: Continue to have a dialogue about bullying and social difficulties, while reminding her that you are there for her, you hear her, and you love her.

School Involvement

Action 1: Get to know the school's bullying policy and key people in the school.

Know Your Daughter "In"ternet and Out!

Action 1: Know your daughter's social scene and ask questions about it to stay informed.

Action 2: Keep tabs on the cell phone.

Action 3: Become Internet savvy.

Chapter 3:
Top Five Talking Points

1. How are things going in school? Who do you sit with at lunch? Are your friends always pretty nice to each other?

2. Is there anyone in your class who you think of as a bully or even anyone who might be hurting other people's feelings? What do you do when you see that happening?

3. I know it can be tough to stick up for someone else, but teasing others, or going along with someone who is teasing others, is not acceptable. I hope you would never purposely try to make anyone feel badly about him or herself.

4. If you heard someone making someone else feel badly, or if someone was making you feel badly, you can always talk to me about it. It is important that you let an adult know that this is going on.

5. I know your privacy is super important to you, but your safety and happiness are my priority. That is why I need to be your friend on Facebook and check out your cell phone from time to time.

Resources for *Internet Safety*

http://www.netsmartz.org/netparents.htm

This is a website run by the National Center for Missing & Exploited Children. It has great information on what parents need to know about Internet safety, definitions of common Internet and web-related terms, products to purchase, and discussion boards.

http://www.wiredsafety.org/parent.html

This website includes a cybercrime tip form, really cool presentations that you could even watch with your daughter about cyberstalking and harassment, and even tips to help you if you find out your child is a cyberbully!

http://kidshealth.org/parent/positive/family/net_safety.html

Kidshealth.org has almost everything about kids on it, so go and look around even if you aren't interested in Internet information. It is also super user-friendly.

http://www.getnetwise.org

This website is set up in a very easy way. There are neat blogs to read, and step-by-step videos that literally guide you through ways to make the Internet safer for your child by doing simple things like changing privacy settings on social media accounts.

http://www.safeteens.com

This is a site for teens, but has a section for parents. It is very teen-friendly and might be a nice resource to share with your daughter and her friends.

http://www.cybertipline.com

This is a website where you can report crimes against children. You can also call 1-800-843-5678 if you would prefer to report by phone.

Non-Internet Resources

Check with your local library, police department, school, or even the county courthouse for seminars, workshops, or experts who know about Internet safety. In many areas the district attorney's office or the attorney general's office have people who are able to give workshops on Internet safety.

FOUR

"Boobies" and More

This chapter comes with a disclaimer: Throughout the chapter, you will see words such as boobs, boobies, and knockers. The sprinkling of such words throughout the chapter is intentional, so that you will get used to these terms. To help the girl in your life, you need to get comfortable talking about breasts, boobs, periods, Aunt Flo, and more. So try to read this chapter without giggling too much or making too many judgments. . . .

Alice sat in baggy clothes with long bangs covering her face and shoulders that were rounded in and hunched. Alice's father was worried that she was so quiet and seemed to have lost a lot of her spunk. In talking to Alice alone, she recounted a moment she shared with her father, "I was sitting on the couch in my nightgown and my Dad looked at me and totally freaked out. He said what I was wearing was inappropriate and to put a sweatshirt on. I didn't know what he was talking about and he yelled at me, saying that my nightgown was see-through and I should cover up. When I went to my room, I realized it was kind of see-through, and I think he could see my chest a little. I didn't mean to offend him and I certainly would have worn something else if I had realized it was see-through. Ever since then, I am so embarrassed to be around him. I try to cover everything up as best I can. I went on a diet, too, and my bras are all too big now, so that is probably a good thing since my chest won't be so noticeable."

Here is a case in which embarrassment on the part of both father and daughter led to a huge misunderstanding, reinforcement that Alice should feel shame about her developing body, and the beginning of an eating disorder. From Alice's perspective, she had gotten ready for bed and was sitting on the couch hanging out with her father. As soon as he angrily directed her to change, she was mortified. Alice felt responsible for embarrassing her father since she believed he thought she knew her nightgown was see-through. This made her feel "dirty" and afraid that her father thought she was showing off her body inappropriately, which led to deep feelings of shame. Alice was also mortified because her father had seen her body through the nightgown. To top it all off, Alice became very anxious and fearful that she would wear the wrong clothes and her father would yell at her again. Alice's solution to this was to wear baggy clothing, stay in her room more, and do anything possible to keep her changing body from changing. Unfortunately for Alice, this meant not eating since it led to a relatively quick decrease in cup size and feelings of control and less shame about her body.

From Dad's perspective, even noticing Alice's body was changing horrified and embarrassed him. He became so anxious when he caught a glimpse of her body through the nightgown that he yelled at her to go change. In that instant, Dad realized he had no control over Alice's changing body and he didn't know how to handle it. He never thought that Alice hadn't noticed how she looked in the nightgown. He even wondered if she was trying to make him uncomfortable, which then made him feel even more concerned about the teenage years ahead. Dad's solution from then on was to pretend that nothing had ever happened and to completely ignore the fact that Alice was changing and growing up.

If you look at both perspectives, there is a lot going on for each person that is the same. Both are struggling to accept the fact that Alice's body is changing. Both feel out of control about the situation. Both are embarrassed and feel shame. Both go to extreme measures to make the situation disappear—Dad by ignoring it, and Alice by wasting away so anything womanly about her is lost.

Poor Alice and poor Dad!! Unfortunately when adults get anxious, they often react with anger because they don't know how to control or fix the situation. This generally backfires because, in the child's mind, an angry reaction means the child has done something wrong or bad to offend the adult. In Alice's case, what she was doing "wrong" was going through puberty—which is not something that is in her, her Dad's, or anyone else's control!

So how do parents and other caregivers deal with the wonders of puberty? How can you be prepared for this event? The first step is easy. Accept that it will happen.

Action 1: Accept that your daughter's body is going to change no matter what you try to do to stop it.

Darn it, this book doesn't have a magic spell that will stop her boobs from growing, her period from coming, or her hormones from raging. So you need to realize that your daughter is going to go through puberty and it is going to be obvious to you, her, and everyone else. It will be like the elephant in the room if you don't address it, and, as the adult, you need to address it without blaming her for it. How do you do that? Find any resource out there that will help. Books, websites, the school nurse or guidance counselor, or even her pediatrician can all be great resources. Even if you are a woman who has gone through puberty, it doesn't hurt to brush up on what actually goes on in the body during that time. Keep in mind that her puberty may be different from yours. It could start earlier or later, bring acne, body odor, big boobs, or big hips. See the resources at the end of the chapter for some starting points on where to look for help.

Action 2: Get comfortable with how her body is going to change by accessing resources such as books or her pediatrician.

Puberty is defined on the National Institutes of Health's website as the time in life when a person becomes sexually mature. For girls, this happens between the ages of nine and fourteen. Although it seems as though the age of puberty is getting younger and younger, an article in *Newsweek* points out that the age of onset in the '60s was between ten and eleven years of age and now it is between ten and ten and a half years of age. This is not a huge difference, but it is still rather curious.

BOOBS

Boobs are a biggie (or rather small in some cases). They are like a sign that states, "I am going through puberty." As if puberty isn't bad enough on its own, girls have to deal with the world knowing they are going through it. Unfortunately, the size of your boobs can actually change how you do things for the rest of your life. A girl with double Ds pretends she no longer wants to figure skate because "I hate it." In reality, she loves skating, but she is embarrassed that her chest is a focal point for anyone watching her skate. A girl with a minimal chest feels less attractive than her friends with more sizable chests, so she starts going further sexually with boys to maintain their interest.

Who has it easier? Neither one! The girls with the bigger boobs are often assumed to be "sluts" simply because they have beacons of sexuality for everyone to see. The flatter-chested girls often end up with nicknames that make fun of their lack of endowment, but are just as terrible.

What can you as a caregiver do to make life with or without boobs a little less horrible? Talk about them. Address their existence and help your daughter learn how to dress them appropriately. An easy way to start the conversation is by suggesting that you go bra shopping. From there, you can explain to her that everyone develops on a completely different time line. Commenting that some girls have huge boobs in fifth grade, but by the time seventh grade rolls around half the class has caught up and the other half is likely to have surpassed her in size, might help her see that boobs are a work in progress and comparing herself to others is an unnecessary stress she should not put on herself. Is she worried that she is too big, or too small? Has anyone made any comments to her or any of her friends? Impress upon her that although boobs get a lot of attention, they are just boobs; the size of them does not define her unless she wants this to happen. Her brain and her other qualities are much more important than her boobs, even if it doesn't always feel that way. If you and she believe that boobs are just boobs, no big deal, this will minimize the possibility that she will feel ashamed of them.

Another tough part about boobs is how to dress them. Depending on the trends of the season, if she has big boobs, she might look like she is trying to be provocative even if she is just trying to wear what is popular. That can get really tricky. This is where the flat-chested girls tend to get away with a little more. Clothes may accentuate their flat-chestedness, but there are so many types of bras to boost or enhance, that they can fake their endowment if they see this as necessary. Girls with larger boobs, however, often struggle with finding ways to minimize the appearance of their breasts. Even when they do, they don't always look appropriate in the trends of the season, which stinks! For the most part, kids want to fit in with their peers, and when something makes them stick out, they can feel ashamed about whatever it is that makes them different. So be creative. Are there ways your daughter can wear trendy clothes without feeling as though she looks like she is drawing attention to her knockers? Help her find a way.

The idea of looking appropriate brings up another issue. What if your daughter thinks she looks totally fine in an outfit (like Alice did in her nightgown), but you look at her and think "Holy moly, where did that cleavage come from? We need to cover it up ASAP!" Like the nightgown incident, this type of situation needs to be addressed with compassion, not with anger or any sort of freak-out on your part. She may think she looks respectable and truly not recognize that she is showing too much skin. You need to approach this kind of problem with caution. Point out that her outfit is a bit revealing, but don't embarrass her or make her self-conscious. One approach is to make a joke about yourself, "Okay, I might be totally old-fashioned and out of the loop, but maybe a tank top under that would be cuter? Not for nothing kiddo, but boys like to look at boobs and I want to make sure you know and they know you are more than just your boobs!! Do I sound totally corny? Do you think I am a big loser?" Make it about you. If you are a female and you had big boobs like her, maybe you can tell a story about not realizing how to handle them when you were younger. If you are not as "blessed" in that area, you can certainly joke about your situation.

Keeping the dialogue light but honest is your best bet. This will hopefully help her to understand that boobs, big, small, lopsided, or whatever, are something all women deal with and nothing to feel shame about. Build awareness, not self-consciousness!

Here is an interesting statistic: According to a story published in 2007, "In the last fifteen years, the average bra size has increased from 34B to 36C."

AND MORE

Here is a reassuring statement: If you can talk about breasts, you can talk about the rest of puberty pretty easily. Okay, pubic hair can be a tough one, too, but boobs are like your initiation into the puberty talk. Facts that need to be addressed include body hair, body odor, hygiene, acne, and menstruation. You should also try to answer any questions your daughter might have, or to make someone available to her who can answer her questions. If she doesn't want to talk to you about it, be grown up enough to find her someone she can talk to, such as the school nurse, a counselor, or her pediatrician.

Action 3: Let her know that she can talk to you about her body. If she is not comfortable doing so, tell her you will help her find someone with whom she will feel comfortable.

THE PHYSICALLY MATURE AND THE PHYSICALLY IMMATURE

Both the mature girl and the immature girl need to know one fact: You are there for her if she needs to talk about puberty or anything else. You might not know all the answers, but you will listen nonjudgmentally, without getting angry or making her feel embarrassed. If she comes to you with a question you think of as embarrassing, imagine how nervous she must have been about asking you and how badly she must want the answer if she is willing to risk asking!

THE IMMATURE GIRL

This is the twelve-year-old who loves her dolls, who is clueless about sexual relationships, and who is in many ways the dream daughter because she isn't scaring the crap out of you yet. She might be the one who is teased about being babyish or not cool enough. If it doesn't faze her, enjoy it. Childhood ends too soon these days and if your daughter has the self-confidence and desire to stay "young," let her do so. What tends to happen, however, is that the social pressures to grow up or at least act more grown-up will start to make her self-conscious and she will doubt herself. Is playing with dolls too babyish? Should she wear different clothes? She likes the ones she has, but Amy said they make her look like she is in fifth grade and she is in sixth grade. She doesn't want them to think she is a baby. . . . Maybe she will put her dolls away except for one and not play with them anymore. . . . Some of this comes with growing up and is very normal. Peer relationships teach us about experiencing new things. Maybe your daughter will become interested in something considered more "mature" and find that she would rather tend to that than to her dolls anyway. What is important during this time of transition is to help her hold on to who she is. Encourage her to be herself. There is no sense in trying to grow up too fast since growing up is inevitable. It isn't like she is going to miss the growing-up boat. Assure her that you will support her no matter when she packs the dolls away.

As the years go on, the immature girl can often be the one who is bullied or taken advantage of, and although holding on to her in this naïve state may seem great to you, it is important to prepare her to stand up for herself. These girls can be the ones who become so frustrated with taunting or social ostracism that they go further than they would like to with a boy to prove a point. Or they drink more to show that they are more grown-up than their peers think. Educating her about peer pressure and giving her tools you will find in the following chapters can help.

THE MATURE GIRL

The mature girl may want to be the immature girl, but, due to circumstances of puberty, she is thrown into the role of the mature girl because she looks older, her body is more developed, or she appears more sophisticated than her peers. These girls tend to make most caregivers nervous. The mature girl's parents might be worried that her curves get her the wrong attention and therefore yell at her about her clothing (like Alice!!!). They might also worry more about relationships and become suspicious of her sexual activity. Caregivers of her friends might worry about the same things and decide it is best for their daughters to stop hanging out with her, just because she comes across as more physically mature than other girls.

These girls are at risk of playing out the stereotype and doing what others think they are doing anyway. They are also at risk of losing out on their childhood. When a girl looks older than she is, the expectations of others change. Even an adult might find it odd for an eight-year-old who looks twelve to be playing with dolls, which is actually normal behavior for an eight-year-old. Mature girls are treated differently by everyone: girls are mean to them and don't like them because they are "slutty" even if they have never entertained the idea of kissing someone; boys are often chatting them up because they are naturally curious about the body that is developing so publicly; and adults often stereotype them as well. A grown man (teacher, coach, or friend's parent) may find he flirts a bit with her because she seems sophisticated. A grown woman (teacher, coach, or friend's parent) may resent her for being physically mature. It is really tough to be a mature girl in a world where people do judge you by your appearance.

The more support she has from you the better. She will need to learn early on how to recognize sexual harassment and how to stick up for herself around her peers. She also will need to learn how to ask for help if an adult is harassing her. She needs your support and not your judgment. You might find that you need to step into situations for her when adults are involved.

Both types of girls need to know that you are there to protect them. Mature, immature, big boobs, no hips, acne, crooked teeth, and hairy chins; you will be there when she needs you.

Action 4: Stick up for her if anyone makes a negative or inappropriate comment about her body.

THE IMPORTANCE OF MEN

Are you a man raising a girl? Are you horrified that she is getting to "that age"? Well, whatever "that age" means, she is going to get there so you better be ready for it. And guess what? You are ready. Don't run screaming at the thought of having to buy tampons. Don't imagine yourself weighed down in the lingerie department by push-up bras and other horrors. What your daughter needs is a man in her life who is man enough to talk to her about the issues of puberty without scarring anyone, or comfortable enough with his own discomfort that he can find someone else great to talk to her about puberty.

Please do not feel any shame if you are not up to having the puberty talk. If you feel really uncomfortable talking to your daughter about puberty, let her know. Don't say, "That period stuff grosses me out; your Aunt Talulah is going to talk to you about it." What you could say is, "Gee, I know it is about that time that we should talk about things like puberty, your period, and stuff like that, but I think it might be helpful for you to talk to a female about it. I've never been through it so it might help to talk to one of your aunts, cousins, or even your doctor. What do you think?" Let her know that you want her to be informed, but you don't know—because of your own lack of experience (not because it freaks you out)—if you are the best person for the job. If you do find her someone to talk to, ask her if it was helpful after they talk. Remind her that if she ever has any questions about puberty that she can ask you. If you don't have the answer, you will find someone who does. Remind her that she can ask you to set up a conversation for her with someone else and you won't ask her questions after the fact.

If you do feel up to having the talk, make sure that you take it seriously. No joking around. Seriously. You might think that stating the obvious, "Well Jenny, since an alien with boobs has taken over your body, I guess we should talk about bra shopping!" is clever. Ha, ha, ha. No, no, no. Not funny! If your idea of talking to her incorporates any jokes, you might be better off handing the responsibility of the conversation to someone else. Just because you feel up to having the conversation does not mean she will feel up to having it with you. Don't be offended. She might be embarrassed about you seeing her as a young woman instead of your little girl. Let her talk to the person with whom she is most comfortable. This isn't about you; it is about her getting the information she needs in a setting where she feels at ease.

Here are some concerns brought up by male caregivers:

"Where is she supposed to put her lady products?" Clean out a drawer in the bathroom, or part of the vanity, and tell her that is her space for storing anything she might need in the bathroom.

"What if she needs tampons? What am I supposed to do? I know I will buy the wrong ones. . . ." Start a habit of writing lists of what you need at the store. Ask her to add to the list whenever she needs something. Keep the list available to her, but not in a place where she would be too embarrassed to add to it (hanging on the fridge = bad; in the junk drawer = good).

"My daughter said she needs bras. What can I do?" Call a local lingerie store (seriously) or a department store and ask if there is someone who would be available to fit your daughter for a bra. Make an appointment and bring her. You are basically just bringing her to an appointment, paying for her purchases, and leaving. You won't have to do a thing.

"My daughter gets really grumpy around her period, but when I point that out she gets even angrier." And that surprises you? No jokes, remember? If she seems cranky, give her the space she needs. If she seems overly cranky or depressed, make an appointment for her to see her doctor and have her doctor talk to her about her moods.

"I feel like my daughter is missing out because she only has me. She doesn't get to bra shop or have the period talk with a mom." The period talk and bra shopping are both totally overrated. Many girls don't want to do either one with their moms anyway, so don't fret.

What is the best thing you can do as a male caregiver? Be respectful of your daughter and the changes her body is experiencing. As uncomfortable as it may be for you to see her thongs in the laundry or to ask her if she needs any tampons, it is probably much more uncomfortable for her. The more at ease you are with everything (even if you have to fake it), the less of a big deal it will seem to her and she will be less likely to be ashamed or embarrassed.

Quick Tips for Men:

1. Don't make jokes about puberty, boobs, periods, pubic hair, hips, or feminine products. Those are off limits.

2. Let her know you are there for her as someone she can talk to personally or someone who will help her find the right person to consult.

3. Find ways of communicating that work for both of you. Have her write down what she needs instead of having to ask for it, or give her an allowance each month that enables her to buy her own products.

4. Don't be offended if she doesn't want to talk to you about puberty. This is about her needs, not yours.

5. Don't be afraid to tell her you are not the expert, but make sure you let her know you will find someone for her who is.

Got it? In a perfect world, your daughter could yell to you from two stories up, "Hey Dad, grab me some super plus tampons at the store, would you? My period is really bad. Oh! And I need new bras, the Cs are too small!" Most people aren't that comfortable, and there is no need to force anyone to become that comfortable. As long as she feels that she has a safe and respectful adult in you and a knowledgeable adult somewhere in her life that she can talk to, she will be just fine—and so will you!

Chapter 4:
Action Recap

Action 1: Accept that your daughter's body is going to change no matter what you try to do to stop it.

Action 2: Get comfortable with how her body is going to change by accessing resources such as books or her pediatrician.

Action 3: Let her know that she can talk to you about her body. If she is not comfortable doing so, tell her you will help her find someone with whom she will feel comfortable.

Action 4: Stick up for her if anyone makes a negative or inappropriate comment about her body.

Chapter 4:
Top Five Talking Points

1. It is probably time we talked a bit about how your body is changing or how your friends' bodies are changing.

2. It is okay to be embarrassed, but I really want you to feel comfortable talking about this. If it isn't me, I won't be offended at all, but I want to find someone with whom you feel comfortable.

3. Everyone is totally different and goes through puberty in different ways, so comparing yourself to others isn't always the best way to judge if what you are going through is normal.

4. Sometimes going through puberty can be really tough. Is there anything you can think of that would make this more comfortable?

5. Believe it or not, I went through puberty once, too, so if you have any questions about how I handled it I would be happy to talk to you about it.

Chapter 4: *Resources*

Web Resources on Puberty:

http://pbskids.org/itsmylife/body/puberty/index.html

Great website!! It has answers to questions from real girls who are anxious about puberty, crossword puzzles on puberty, and is very kid-friendly.

http://www.healthychildren.org/English/ages-stages/gradeschool/
puberty/Pages/default.aspx:

Very long website name, but worth a peek. This is the American Academy of Pediatrics site for parents and families and is more suitable for parents looking for information to help them talk to their daughters about puberty and get good solid facts.

http://kidshealth.org/

This is a great website all around, but one of the coolest things about it is if you search a term—such as "puberty"—not only will awesome resources appear, but also those resources are coded as "P" for "parent," "K" for "kid," "T" for "teen," and so on. This way you know for whom the article is most appropriate.

Great Books on Puberty

Mayle, Peter. *Where Did I Come From?* New York, NY: Lyle Stuart, 2000.

Mayle, Peter. *What's Happening to Me?* New York, NY: Lyle Stuart, 2000.

FIVE

Sexual Harassment

Sexual harassment affects girls every day. Sometimes they don't even notice it is happening, and sometimes the harasser doesn't recognize that what he or she is doing is considered harassment. Similar to bullying, there are people who fit into the "standby" category. These are boys, girls, men, women, teachers, parents—anyone—who don't do anything to stop harassment when they encounter it personally or when they witness it happening to someone else. Read on for examples of outright harassment, hidden harassment, and how to help your daughter recognize it and do something about it.

What is sexual harassment? On the United States Equal Employment Opportunity Commission (EEOC) website, sexual harassment includes unwelcome sexual advances, requests for sexual favors, and other verbal or physical conduct of a sexual nature when this conduct explicitly or implicitly affects an individual's employment, unreasonably interferes with an individual's work performance, or creates an intimidating, hostile, or offensive work environment. But work is not the only place where sexual harassment occurs. One of the best descriptions of sexual harassment in school comes from the Equal Rights Advocates:

"It is different from flirting, playing around, or other types of behavior that you enjoy or welcome. Sexual harassment can be requests for sexual favors or unwelcome sexual behavior that is bad enough or happens often enough to make you feel uncomfortable, scared or confused and that interferes with your schoolwork or your ability to participate in extracurricular activities or attend classes."

The key in both settings is that it is something that makes the person being harassed feel uncomfortable.

What are the ways in which someone can be sexually harassed? Sexual harassment can be verbal, meaning it can be someone saying harassing things either directly or indirectly to or about the person; physical, like being touched in a way the person doesn't like; or visual, shown pictures or images that make the person uncomfortable. Unfortunately, it is getting easier to sexually harass others because of all the ways of posting sexual content on the Internet. Texting or "sexting" is getting quite popular. This is getting a great deal of coverage lately in the media because of people not knowing how to appropriately punish kids for posting or sending sexual pictures or messages. The only way many states had to take action was to charge kids as distributing child pornography. This is a bit harsh as most kids were taking pictures of themselves and willingly passing them around. Many states are looking to create different laws to address these cases.

So what is the big deal if kids are willingly sending them? The person who is receiving the picture is the one who is in a position of being harassed. This is something to really keep in mind as a parent.

Your daughter may send a suggestive picture of herself to the boy she likes only to find out that he was really uncomfortable receiving it and told someone he felt as though she was harassing him. She might show her friend a picture that someone sent her, only to make her friend feel uncomfortable and therefore harassed.

This brings us to a touchy part of this subject; who can harass whom? Sexual harassment can happen between peers, by a teacher, administrator, coach, boss, coworker, or any other person. It can happen between people of the same sex or the opposite sex. It can happen between friends or enemies. Your daughter could harass someone. Your daughter's friend could harass someone. Someone could harass your daughter. As a parent, similar to the bullying situation, you need to know any potential role your daughter could play in sexual harassment so you can best educate her and safeguard her against participating in any role. The sexting examples from above are good examples of how your daughter could harass someone without realizing it. She could send a picture of herself rather innocently in her mind, only to totally offend the receiver of the picture. She could also offend a friend by sharing pictures someone sent her. These are important things to talk to her about so she understands that it is easier than she may realize to put someone else in an uncomfortable position.

Now that you have a bit of an overview on sexual harassment, let's look at the two types of sexual harassment: Quid Pro Quo and Hostile Environment.

QUID PRO QUO

In Latin, quid pro quo means "this for that." Sexual harassment occurs when a teacher or school employee offers you a better grade or treats you better if you do something sexual. It could also be a threat to lower your grade or treat you worse than other students if you refuse to go along with a request for a sexual favor. For example, if your teacher says, "I'll give you an 'A' if you go out with me," or "I'll fail you in this class if you don't have sex with me," this is sexual harassment.

HOSTILE ENVIRONMENT

This type of sexual harassment occurs when unwanted sexual touching, comments, and/or gestures are so bad or occur so often that they interfere with your schoolwork, make you feel uncomfortable or unsafe at school, or prevent you from participating in or benefiting from a school program or activity. This type of harassment does not have to involve a threat or promise of benefit in exchange for a sexual favor. The harassment can be from a teacher, school officials, or other students.

Both of these definitions are taken from the Equal Rights Advocates website. The site defines these different types so well and in such great context, you could easily share these definitions with your daughter verbatim and then have a conversation about different things that could be seen as sexual harassment.

Action 1: Educate your daughter on the definition of sexual harassment and the different types of sexual harassment. Find out if she has encountered anything like this.

Why does this subject seem so tricky? Wouldn't my daughter just tell me if she felt she was being sexually harassed? Wouldn't the school do something if they thought she was being sexually harassed? Not necessarily. This is a tricky subject at this time because kids are getting more curious, anxious, uncertain, freaked out, and interested in sex and their bodies. They are also trying to fit in with their peers more than with their parents, so doing things their friends do seems like the cool thing to do even if it makes them a little uncomfortable.

Would your daughter tell you that something was making her uncomfortable? Not always, especially if she thought it could hurt her social life, social standing, make you angry, or affect her grades. Also, she might not really know how to voice that she is uncomfortable with something. For example, Meredith had a great job at a local coffee place. The boss was "kind of creepy, but nice enough." When asked to describe how he was creepy, Meredith would get flustered. Her assignment for the next week was to take note of when he seemed creepiest and mark it down somewhere so she could figure out what there was about him that bothered her.

Here is what her list looked like:

- ☑ Bill told me my shirt looked nice and brought out the blue in my eyes. He said it was his favorite shirt and bet I made more tips when I wore it.
- ☑ Bill told me I could have another shift since I wore his favorite shirt again.
- ☑ Bill told me it looked like my gym membership was working because I looked really fit.
- ☑ He suggested I wear shorts instead of pants now that it was getting warmer out.

When Meredith presented her list, she said she felt like "an ass" because he was probably just trying to be nice to her and she was creeped out for no reason. After all, he was really nice and knew she needed extra money because her Dad had lost his job. One question posed to Meredith was, "What's the deal with the shirt? It seems like he really likes it and that makes you uncomfortable. If it makes you so uncomfortable, why do you wear it?"

Meredith replied, "He is so much nicer to me when I wear that shirt that it is worth wearing. He always rubs my shoulders when I wear it—which is kind of gross, but he always gives me extra shifts and will put an extra couple of dollars in my tip jar that I get to take home after my shift. An extra couple of tips does make a difference with everything going on with my dad. I feel like it is worth the creepiness for the extra money. It isn't like he is hurting me or making me do things with him. Plus, it is kind of my fault since I wear that shirt. If I didn't wear it he might not say stuff, but then I wouldn't get more shifts and that would stink."

What an innocent take on the interactions. Meredith definitely felt uncomfortable, but even when asked to take note of what transpired, she had a really difficult time explaining it. The shoulder rubbing came up as an afterthought—most likely because it happened so frequently that she was used to it. Meredith was hesitant to talk about this situation since her job was helping her family in their time of need, and part of her was feeling like it was her fault that he treated her this way. She also voiced concerns that her friend who also worked there would think she was overreacting and a drama queen, and that her mother would think she was "a slut" for wearing the shirt. What a disaster! In dealing with this situation, Meredith needed to hear that there was reason for her to feel that he was being "creepy" and to listen to her gut. She was not overreacting. What her boss was doing was wrong and inappropriate. She also needed to hear, and be reminded over and over and over again, that this was not her fault—not at all!

Situations like this require a lot of patience. They are often hard to find out about because kids usually aren't really sure what they should be comfortable and uncomfortable with, and they often don't know how to speak up for themselves. Even if your daughter is not experiencing sexual harassment, letting her know that she can talk to you about people who make her feel uncomfortable or "creepy" is one way of opening the lines of communication. Another way is to occasionally ask her how things are going at work and at school? Is anyone bothering her or making her feel uncomfortable?

Action 2: Open the lines of communication. Make sure your daughter knows she can talk to you about situations that make her uncomfortable.

Now that you know what harassment is and why it is so hard for kids to talk about, you need to know what to do about it if it does happen to your daughter. Below are different ways of reacting to a situation as a parent—some good, some not so good. Once you read through them, we will pick apart the last scenario in detail:

Jenna used to be a straight A student in math. Suddenly her grades tanked, so her mom asked what was going on. Here are some examples of how to and how not to react:

Scenario 1:

Jenna is sitting in the living room sulking.

"What is going on in math, Jenna?" Mom sounds annoyed.

"I hate it. John's in that class." Jenna flips on the television.

Mom turns it off.

"Listen, this is serious. If you fail math, you will have to go to summer school, your GPA will take a nosedive, and you won't be in advanced classes anymore. You can't tell me you are going to let an ex-boyfriend affect your future like that. A few months from now, you won't even care about him."

"Oh, well." Jenna looks at the wall, trying to keep the tears in her eyes from pouring down her face.

"Jenna!!!" Mom sounds super annoyed, not noticing the tears, but annoyed that Jenna won't make eye contact.

"I just hate the teacher, okay? I will try and do better." Jenna gets up and goes to her room.

Oh, no! Mom is mad Jenna isn't doing well, and instead of looking at Jenna's body language, or really listening to her, Mom just focuses on what will happen if Jenna continues to do poorly in class. Mom discounts the effect Jenna's ex might be having on her class performance. Mom totally misses the boat.

Scenario 2:

Jenna is sitting in the living room sulking.

Her parents walk in. Dad takes the remote since Jenna often turns on the TV when she doesn't want to talk.

Jenna sighs.

Mom stands off to the side. Dad sits down, facing Jenna like an interrogator. "Jenna, you are failing math. This is unacceptable. What is going on?" he demands.

Jenna starts bouncing her leg up and down and fiddles with her hands.

"I guess it is just really hard this year."

"Well then, we will get you a tutor," Dad announces. He looks at Mom, "Will you call the school tomorrow and get the name of some tutors?"

Mom nods her head in agreement.

Jenna rolls her eyes.

Dad notices, "Annoying you, are we? What else is going on? All you do is sulk around."

Jenna looks at her Mom pleadingly. Mom smiles meekly.

"Some kids are bothering me in that class."

Dad puffs his chest out. "Who?! What are they doing?!"

"It's the boys in the class. A few of them hold up signs rating how I look when I walk in."

Dad is fuming. "Is this that idiot, John!??? Give me your phone. I am calling him right now. Then I will go to his house and straighten this out with his father."

Jenna is horrified. "Dad, NO! I can handle it. They haven't been as bad lately. I am sure it will stop soon."

"Well, what is the teacher doing about it?" Dad demands.

"Nothing. She told me to ignore it. I shouldn't have let it distract me."

"That teacher is an idiot. She should kick them out of class. If this doesn't get better by the end of the week, we are going up to that school and demanding that they switch your class. What they all need is a good punch in the face."

Oh, dear. Dad cares about Jenna, but yikers! Can you imagine? Thinking they deserve a punch in the face is one thing, but saying it or even remotely suggesting you might follow through with it is a bad idea and one that will prevent your daughter from opening up to you in the future!

Scenario 3:

Jenna is sitting in the living room sulking.

"Hey Jenna, what's up with math?" Mom sounds worried and genuinely curious.

"I hate it. John's in that class." Jenna flips on the television.

Mom sits down next to her, "That stinks. Can we talk for a few minutes before you watch TV?"

Jenna reluctantly shuts off the television and sulkily looks at Mom.

"Is it math or is it John? I know math can get pretty tough. I also know that breaking up is pretty tough."

Tears start to roll down Jenna's face.

"The work is fine. I can do the work, and I am happy I broke up with John. Whenever I walk into math class, John and the two boys next to him hold up pieces of paper with a number between one and ten on them."

Mom looks baffled. "I am confused. Why are they holding up numbers?"

"They rate how I look every day. It is so awful!! I know I shouldn't care if I am a one or a ten because they are jerks, but I worry all day about what they are going to hold up, and then I am self-conscious all through class that I look too ugly or that my shirt is too tight. It bugs me all day!"

"Oh Jenna! Did you tell the teacher?" Mom sounds concerned, not angry.

"Yes but she told me to just ignore them."

"What does she do when she sees the signs?"

"She ignores them." Jenna slumps back, looking defeated.

Mom pauses a minute, "Well Jenna, this isn't okay. This is harassment. We have to figure out the best way to address this. What would you think of me going to talk to the teacher or your guidance counselor?"

Hooray! Mom listened, appreciated that John, the ex, is in the class and is probably having an effect on Jenna's performance, also appreciated that math is tough, admitted to Jenna she was confused about what the boys were doing, told Jenna what they were doing wasn't right, let Jenna know she wanted to do something about it but wanted Jenna's help in how to best address the issue. Yay Mom!

The last example shows a family whose lines of communication are open. Instead of jumping to conclusions or immediately getting angry about the grade or the harassment, Jenna's mom asks Jenna what is going on. This might sound obvious, but many parents skip that step! Because Mom is open to hearing Jenna's story, she ends up hearing more details about what is going on in Jenna's class.

Action 3: Be patient and ask your daughter what is going on before getting angry or jumping to conclusions.

Jenna's mom also includes Jenna in the decision to talk to the guidance counselor or teacher. Now, Jenna's mom will make the ultimate decision, but she puts it out there first before just telling Jenna what she is going to do. So many times parents make decisions for their daughters without at least checking in with them first. You may end up disagreeing anyway, but first hear what she has to say. Jenna may say, "Gee, I am really uncomfortable talking to my guidance counselor. Do you think we could talk to the assistant headmaster instead?" This is a totally reasonable request, and you wouldn't have known to do that if you just bulldozed into the school and talked to whomever you thought was the best choice.

Action 4: Let your daughter be a part of the decision-making process when it comes to confronting or dealing with the situation.

Let's go over the roles played out in the situation. Who is the harasser? Jenna's ex and his friends. Their harassment creates a hostile environment for Jenna that has gotten so bad that her schoolwork and self-confidence are suffering.

Who is the standby? The teacher? Well, she is actually worse than a standby since Jenna has brought her discomfort to her attention. She is an ignorer and enabler because she is letting this go on. Once a child asks an adult for help and the adult does not help, the child learns that the adult is not to be trusted and will then be reluctant to ask another adult for help. So is she really just a standby or is she even more of a problem? More of a problem! She is the adult in the classroom who is supposed to make sure that students feel safe and respected. So then who is the standby? Perhaps her peers—their role is similar to those standing by when someone is being bullied.

And now, here is a tricky question; who is being harassed? Jenna is being harassed, but is anyone else being indirectly harassed? Probably. Imagine being one of the other girls in class. They are probably worried that they will be next, or that people are judging them already. Imagine how distracting it is for everyone in the class and how self-conscious many of them would be about how they look, just knowing that this kind of judgment is happening. This can take her peers out of the standby category and place them in the harassed category.

Action 5: Think about all the players in these situations and how they are affected.

How can you tell if your daughter is being sexually harassed? This is a tough one. As mentioned above, she might not tell you. You also may never be in a place where she is being harassed. If she works after school but usually gets home before you do, you probably won't see her much at her workplace. If it is happening in school or in an after-school program, you may not be privy to that situation either. So what can you do? Follow Action 1 and Action 2—educate your daughter and keep the lines of communication open! Also, looking back at the scenario above, Jenna was throwing out some signs that something was not right. She was sulking and avoiding her parents. Her grades were going down and she was upset. These are all signs that something is up. So take notice of your daughter and any changes in her mood or actions. These changes don't necessarily mean that she is being sexually harassed, but they could mean that she is struggling with something. If you do feel as though something is off, talk to her about it in a nonjudgmental way. Don't just assume she is being a "typical" girl, hitting puberty, or being lazy. There could very well be more to it. Any changes in mood, habits like sleeping and eating, socializing, energy, or motivation should always be discussed.

Action 6: Address any changes in mood, habits, energy, or motivation in a nonjudgmental and open way.

YOUR DAUGHTER HAS BEEN OR IS BEING HARASSED

What if you find out your daughter is or was being sexually harassed? Discuss it with her and determine how you will handle it. If it is currently going on, protect her from the situation so she does not need to face more harassment. If it is occurring at her job, but you haven't figured out how to best handle it, call her in sick for a few days until you do figure it out. If it is occurring at school, find out if she can do her work in the office or in a neutral setting so she is not subjected to more harassment.

Decide what you can do to assure that the harassment stops. If it is a situation with a peer that is occurring at school, the school counselors and administration should be able to help diffuse the situation. If it is a situation with an adult, or if the harassment has reached a severe level, you may decide you need to involve law enforcement. No matter what your decision, do try and be as level-headed as possible about it. Punching someone in the face could feel great in the moment, but your daughter will then have to live with everyone knowing her parent has an anger issue. She could be mortified, and she may be harassed about her parent's anger issue!

Do keep her feelings and wishes in mind, but remember you are the adult and the ultimate decision will be yours. It needs to be the decision that protects your daughter physically and emotionally. Make sure your daughter has someone to talk to about the problem. It could be you, your partner, a sibling, a counselor, anyone. Check in on her self-esteem and any feelings of shame. Confront those feelings right away. Feelings of shame can stay with her and build, especially if she continues to be harassed, and potentially lead to lower self-esteem. Nip those feelings in the bud and encourage her to stay strong.

Action 1: Handle yourself with dignity:

☑ Control your emotions.

☑ Discuss the situation.

☑ Assure her she does not have to go back to the situation.

☑ Listen to your daughter's needs and thoughts.

☑ Decide how to handle it.

☑ Set your daughter up with someone to talk to.

☑ Continue to check in with her to make sure she is feeling strong and not feeling shame.

YOUR DAUGHTER IS HARASSING OR DID HARASS SOMEONE

What if your daughter is the harasser? Take a deep breath and get support for yourself. Similar to bullying, you need to take care of it immediately and find any support you can to help educate her on sexual harassment and the consequences. Do not tolerate this behavior, but do support her when she makes positive changes and decisions. Make sure she understands what harassment is and what can be considered harassment. In some cases, harassment to one person could be flirting to another. Make sure she understands this.

No matter what her involvement, this is another subject that brings up the importance of being that annoying parent who checks out his or her daughter's Internet activity and texting conversations. It is important to know what she puts out there about herself and what others put out there about her. If you don't monitor her activity, you won't know what is going on and that puts her at risk of making a stupid mistake.

Chapter 5:
Action Recap

Action 1: Educate your daughter on the definition of sexual harassment and the different types of sexual harassment. Find out if she has encountered anything like this.

Action 2: Open the lines of communication. Make sure your daughter knows she can talk to you about situations that make her uncomfortable.

Action 3: Be patient and ask your daughter what is going on before getting angry or jumping to conclusions.

Action 4: Let your daughter be a part of the decision-making process when it comes to confronting or dealing with the situation.

Action 5: Think about all the players in these situations and how they are affected.

Action 6: Address any changes in mood, habits, energy, or motivation in a nonjudgmental and open way.

Your Daughter Has Been or Is Being Harassed

Action 1: Handle yourself with dignity:
- ☑ Control your emotions.
- ☑ Discuss the situation.
- ☑ Assure her she does not have to go back to the situation.
- ☑ Listen to your daughter's needs and thoughts.
- ☑ Decide how to handle it.
- ☑ Set your daughter up with someone to talk to.
- ☑ Continue to check in with her to make sure she is feeling strong and not feeling shame.

Chapter 5:
Top Five Talking Points

1. Sexual harassment is anything sexual in nature that makes you feel uncomfortable and unable to do what you need to do at work, school, sports, or other activities. This includes sending suggestive text messages or pictures.

2. If you are being sexually harassed it isn't your fault, and I am not going to think that it is because of something you are doing.

3. If you are being sexually harassed it is important you talk to me about it, and we can figure out how to solve the issue together.

4. It is also important to make sure you aren't making anyone uncomfortable with your own actions, such as sending e-mails or posting things on Facebook that are sexual in nature.

5. If you are feeling any shame or embarrassment about the issue that went on, we can find you someone to talk to—it might really help, and I want to be sure this doesn't affect your self-esteem.

SIX

I Kissed a Girl, and a Boy, and Then a Girl . . .

"I like this girl and I kissed her. Does that mean I am bi forever? Should I tell my friends I like girls? What if I like boys, too? I still think Alex is really hot, and there is a new boy in my class who is hot, too, and I think I still have feelings for my ex-boyfriend. But kissing Cammie was really exciting. It made my stomach all fluttery. But I don't even know if I 'like her like her' or if I just like her." Lindsay was feeling totally confused.

Sexuality can be a tough one. Kids seem to be getting more and more involved, and at younger and younger ages. Many adults reminisce about childhood relationships that were relatively straightforward. A boy dated a girl, and they usually dated exclusively. She wore his varsity sweater or ring. There were no "friends with benefits" or threesomes captured on cell phones. Girls didn't kiss girls just to impress the boy that they liked or to be as cool as the actresses on their favorite television shows. Groups of friends didn't sleep with each other with as much ease as kids do now, or share boyfriends or girlfriends.

What has changed? We are now more accepting of other types of dating situations aside from a boy dating a girl. Thankfully, many kids truly seem open to their gay, bisexual, lesbian, transgendered, and undecided peers. The fact that kids are accepting each other is something that should continue and spread to the adults around them if it hasn't already. Hopefully, today's kids don't feel as much pressure to conform to a stereotype as kids in prior years may have felt.

One thing that needs to be made clear, however, is that this acceptance is *not the cause* of kids becoming more sexually active or more promiscuous. Just because kids accept their gay friends, does not mean that they will then experiment or make decisions that seem risky or hypersexualized.

Unfortunately, at the same time that our culture has started to accept people for who they are and to embrace differences, it seems as though folks are becoming a bit racier. "Whale tails" are the norm, "tramp stamps" have became common, and teenagers seem to be flaunting their sexuality in any way that they can. Access to sexual images is no longer denied by a PG-13 or R rating; kids have access to sexual images on their cell phones and computers. Sex is everywhere; and messages about it are very mixed. We will discuss sex as sex later, but for now, it's important to appreciate that the mixed messages kids are getting about sex seem to be quite confusing to them. Kids seem confused about labeling themselves as gay, lesbian, bisexual, transgendered, or undecided. Not only do they struggle with how to label themselves, but also they seem confused about what those words really mean. As far as experimenting with different sexual experiences, girls especially seem damned if they do and damned if they don't. There is so much discussion about girls kissing girls and how "hot" guys think this is, while at the same time, a girl who does it is considered promiscuous or slutty. To make things even more confusing, a girl who is truly interested in other girls is shunned in many ways. We need to help kids sort these things out and understand the motivations behind their experimentation.

How can we help them with their sexuality and the discovery of their sexual orientation? We must make sure that we are open to the discussion and ready for any curve balls such as, "Mom, I don't like boys. I like girls. I think . . . " Most parents don't prepare themselves for their kids to be anything but straight. Many kids are not straight. As a parent, it is important that you find a way to be okay with it if your child is not straight. You might not find out when she is eleven; she might not tell you until she is thirty. But preparing yourself now to be open to such curve balls certainly won't hurt. Think about it. Would it bother you? Would you be able to accept her and not freak out when she tells you? If not, it is important to address this either by doing some soul-searching on your own or by speaking with a counselor. No matter how hard you try, you will not control your child's sexuality or sexual orientation. What is it that would bother you if your daughter was a lesbian or bisexual? Would you be worried that she wouldn't have children? Would you worry that kids would tease her and that her life would be more difficult than if she were straight? Would you be disappointed? You may be thinking, "Who cares, as long as she is happy!" If so, this is great! But there are many kind and well-meaning parents out there who would really struggle with it. If you are uncomfortable with the idea, the first step toward getting more comfortable with it is recognizing your own discomfort and tracing its source or sources. As a caring parent, it really is important to be ready for those unexpected pitches and able to catch them without falling over or dropping them.

Action 1: Make sure you address your own fears and discomforts about sexual orientation.

To encourage comfort in your child when it comes to sexual orientation, creating a sexually neutral home environment is key. Many parents tease their children when they are as young as preschoolers about their boyfriends and girlfriends, or the crushes they have on teachers of the opposite sex. It would be rare for a parent to comment to her female preschooler that Jenny is cute and they should be girlfriends. It isn't that this teasing is wrong or setting kids up to be confused as they get older; it is just that it sets a picture in their heads of what is "right" and what is "wrong." When really, what is "right" is that they grow up to be happy, healthy, and well-adjusted—no matter what their sexual orientation. Right? So don't get crazy and worried about everything you say, but as your daughter gets older, asking her if there are any cute boys in her class could be replaced by a question such as, "Are you interested in anyone in your class?" This at least takes the assumption that your child is straight out of the question. Be cognizant of how others in the house speak of sexual orientation as well. Does your son refer to something he doesn't like as "gay"? Does your partner comment that lesbian couples are weird? Address the way others speak. They may not even realize they could potentially be insulting someone. This also goes for your daughter. If she is speaking about others in a derogatory or judgmental way, point it out and inform her that your house is one that is open and friendly, and that talking that way is not acceptable. Talking in a more sexually neutral way could encourage your daughter to talk to you about questions she may have about her sexual orientation. At the very least, she will know that there is no pressure for her to fit into the straight category and that your household is an open and nonjudgmental place for her to bring friends no matter what their sexual orientation.

Action 2: Create a sexually neutral household that is safe for your daughter and her friends.

> What if I just can't accept it or if someone in my household cannot accept it? I still love my daughter, but the thought of her being gay, lesbian, bisexual, or anything but straight seems wrong to me and I don't know that I can handle it.

Luckily, there is plenty of help out there for people who struggle with this issue. You can start by looking into counseling or looking for your local Parents, Families and Friends of Lesbians and Gays (PFLAG).

What we need to do to be available to our girls is to understand what they mean by sexuality and sexual orientation. Many kids talk about their sexuality as if that is their sexual orientation, so be prepared to ask your daughter if she is talking about sex in general or if she is talking about how she defines or labels herself sexually.

Many girls are entering therapy and expressing confusion about whether or not they are lesbian or bisexual by the age of twelve. Why are they worried about it? It's on their minds because their peers are asking them what they are, what they have done sexually, or teasing them about their sexuality. For example, Lindsay had a crush on a girlfriend of hers and a few boys at the same time. She was focused on how to label herself as a way of coming up with which one to like best. "Well if I am straight, then obviously I should like Alex because he is the hottest boy, but if I am a lesbian, I should totally go for Cammie. But if I am bi, which is what I think I must be, I am stuck being confused. Am I allowed to go out with both of them if I am a bisexual? When am I supposed to go out with boys and when am I supposed to go out with girls?"

Lindsay was such a thinker that she was thinking herself nutty. What she needed to do was to focus not on the label, but on who she liked and why. Taking labels out of it made it easier for her to decide which person she liked based on their personalities. Kids need help with this stuff. If you can't help your daughter, find someone who can. In Lindsay's case, the decision was really confusing to her. Trying to choose was making her quite frustrated and anxious about who she was, when really, all she needed to do was figure out who she liked best. So if your daughter is struggling with her sexuality, try to reduce her anxiety by reminding her that she is who she is and that won't change just because of the person she likes. If she is feeling very anxious about it, she could talk to a professional or join a support group. If she is feeling pressured to know her sexual orientation when she hasn't figured it out yet, remind her that she doesn't need to tell people what she is, or what she is thinking. It is okay to be confused for a while. Remind her that she doesn't need to post her persuasion on her Facebook account. She doesn't even need to write that she is undecided. She can simply leave it blank.

Action 3: Remind your daughter that she doesn't need to fit herself into any one label. She can just be herself, and like, or "like like" people based on who they are, not on how she has defined herself.

What if your daughter knows without a doubt that she is gay? Well, then she can label herself as she sees fit. She can take the lead—with a lot of help from you. You might want to ask her, "How would you like me to refer to you? Do you prefer the term gay? Lesbian? Do you prefer I don't refer to it at all? Who do you want to know about this? Is there anyone you are nervous about letting know?" If your daughter is ready to put herself into a defined category, then your support is very important. But it is important that you support her in the way she wants to be supported. That is why it is so important to ask her questions, and let her tell you what she wants. You may also have some insight into family members who might not react favorably, or the dangers of posting it on social media sites. Talk to her about how she wants to handle people knowing or not knowing. No matter what her sexual orientation, including straight as an arrow, she does not need to share it with anyone. This seems to be one area where kids are getting a bit confused. But it really isn't anyone else's business.

Action 4: Accept her label if she wants one and follow her lead on how she would like to let people know, if in fact she does want to let people know.

Months after Lindsay muddled through her dilemma, she was back with another dilemma, "Well, I don't think I am bisexual anymore. I have only kissed other girls, and doing anything else with them freaks me out. I really don't want to do anything more with them. Cammie is going to hate me forever if I tell her that I am straight, but she seems to be way more into doing more stuff with me than I want to do. I think I was just experimenting, and I think the experiment is over. I really only like boys. Cammie made me promise I was into her for real and I really thought I was, but now I see that I just thought it was kind of cool to try it. I do really love Cammie, but I love her as my friend. I don't know what to do."

She was in a bit of a pickle, and this is often where kids who experiment find themselves. When they experiment, they often don't think they are only experimenting. They could truly love the person they are kissing or with whom they are being even more sexually active, but actually only love that person as a friend. If both parties agree that they were experimenting, they will probably both shrug it off and continue their friendship. If only one feels this way, however, it makes the situation dicey. The girl who decides she is not a lesbian has more of a support system to go back to—perhaps a relieved family, straight friends, and the comforts of a more socially acceptable way of life. But the girl who is still confused, and may be realizing that she is bisexual or gay, is often left feeling a bit deserted and hurt. She is more likely to feel vulnerable and used, she may have less support from family and friends, and although we are a more accepting society lately, she is still less socially accepted.

So what should a girl who realizes she was just experimenting do? Lindsay ended up having a great conversation with Cammie. She let her know how badly she felt and how much she did love and treasure Cammie as her friend. Cammie was sad. She was angry for a few days, but she ended up realizing how important their friendship was for her as well. Cammie also realized that this girl was her biggest supporter. She decided to accept her fully for who she was. These thirteen-year-olds had an easier time being honest with each other than many adults, and they were really able to process the whole situation.

This is not always the case. Many times one of the parties is mortified by what transpired, and so afraid that people will find out and judge them that the party then spreads rumors about the other person involved or denies any involvement with that person. This only creates shame and hurt. If your daughter is involved in a situation where she changes her mind about her sexuality or someone she has been with does this, you need to be there to support her. Don't judge her, but really listen to how she is managing. Encourage her to deal with it in as kind and respectful a way as possible. Blabbing about other people's business even if she was involved in it is not okay, and it is unfair to the other person.

To avoid this sort of thing happening, talking to your daughter about her motivation behind experimenting could be helpful. Is it because it is "cool"? Is she curious? Did someone tell her they thought it was sexy? You might be surprised at what she tells you. Look at Britney Spears and Madonna—their kiss kept people talking for years. But what did it really mean? Were they in love with each other? Did they do it to be cool? How did their fans come to understand it?

Action 5: If your daughter does "experiment," talk to her about her motivation and be there for her no matter what the outcome. There is no shame in being confused. Encourage her to handle the end of the relationship kindly and with compassion for the other party—just as she should handle the end of any relationship!

Common questions, concerns, and statements girls are often too embarrassed to vocalize and the responses you might use:

1. If I am a lesbian, then I won't ever have to worry about getting hurt or pregnant because girls are nicer and they can't get me pregnant.

   True, girls cannot get you pregnant. But, they can hurt you just as badly as any boy, so if that is why you are not dating boys, you might want to at least reconsider. Anyone can be mean in a relationship. Anyone can be nice in a relationship. The important thing is to find someone who is nice.

2. If I am dating a boy, but I am bisexual, and I hook up with a girl while I am with the boy, is that really cheating since I didn't make out with another boy?

   This is a conversation you should have at the beginning of a relationship with a person you are dating. It seems that the issue here is not really about being bisexual, but instead about being anxious about committing to one person.

3. I totally hooked up with a girl in my class to impress this guy. Now he thinks I am a slut. He told me he wouldn't go out with me because he would never know if I was thinking about him or a girl when we were together. I didn't even want to hook up with her, and now everyone talks about me.

Unfortunately, what is done is done, but it won't haunt you forever. What you need to figure out here is why you felt that doing anything sexual was a good way to impress a guy—especially if it was something you didn't want to do. If *anyone* encourages you to do something sexual that you don't want to do, you should take a break from that relationship and consider if this is someone who really cares about you or not.

Chapter 6:
Action Recap

Action 1: Make sure you address your own fears and discomforts about sexual orientation.

Action 2: Create a sexually neutral household that is safe for your daughter and her friends.

Action 3: Remind your daughter that she doesn't need to fit herself into any one label. She can just be herself, and like, or "like like" people based on who they are, not on how she has defined herself.

Action 4: Accept her label if she wants one and follow her lead on how she would like to let people know, if in fact she does want to let people know.

Action 5: If your daughter does "experiment," talk to her about her motivation and be there for her no matter what the outcome. There is no shame in being confused. Encourage her to handle the end of the relationship kindly and with compassion for the other party—just as she should handle the end of any relationship!

Chapter 6:
Top Five Talking Points

1. I know you have started dating here and there, and I just want you to know that who you date is your decision, boy or girl. The most important thing to me is that he or she is nice to you and treats you with respect.

2. If you are confused or have questions about sexuality, like how to tell if you really like boys or really like girls, I would be happy to talk to you about it, or have you talk to someone you are comfortable with.

3. No matter who you are dating, sometimes everyone makes a mistake—kisses the wrong person, goes a bit too far. I know it can seem like the end of the world, but it won't be. People will forget about it eventually as long as you don't keep doing things you wish you hadn't in hindsight. So, before you experiment, or do anything sexual, pause for a second and think, "Is this really something I want to be doing?"

4. I saw on your Facebook account that you have categorized yourself as bisexual. There is absolutely nothing wrong with that, just keep an open mind. You don't need to categorize yourself as anything but you. As the years go on, you may recognize you are truly bi, you might recognize you are a lesbian, you might recognize you are straight. Don't feel pressure to define yourself if you aren't ready to do so yet.

5. I don't ever want you to feel like I don't want you to be bi or lesbian. I want you to be happy being you, and whatever that means—unless it is harmful to you—I will support you.

Chapter 6: *Resources*

http://www.pflag.org
Parents, Families and Friends of Lesbians and Gays (PFLAG) is a national
nonprofit organization. Their website basically has all the information
you could need and then some.

http://www.advocatesforyouth.org/
This is a cool website that has tons of information on advocacy for kids and
how to get involved. There is a section on GLBTQ (Gay, Lesbian, Bisexual,
Transgendered, and Questioning). It includes resources for parents and
professionals, plus has lots of good information about youth overall.

SEVEN

Sex

Potentially one of the toughest chapters to read, this is a must for every parent. It is hard to hear that your daughter is going to have sex and that it could be soon, but that is the truth. Maybe not by the time she leaves junior high, but if she is not having it in high school, she at least knows kids who are and may have friends who are. It can't hurt to educate yourself on the topic, even if you aren't ready to hear that your daughter may have thought about sex.

Here's an example of how not to react:

Eleven-year-old Shea said to me, "I asked my mom a question about sex and she made me wait and ask my dad. I think she should have answered it herself, but she says I am wrong."

"What was the question?" I asked.

Shea's mother shook her head in embarrassment.

"I wanted to know what a boner was. We are learning about sex in school, and one kid said he had a boner before and everyone laughed. I didn't get what they were laughing about. I laughed anyway so I didn't look stupid though."

"So did anyone tell you what it was?"

"My dad said it is something that happens to adult men and nothing for me to worry about now."

"What did your mom say when you asked her?"

Shea's mom shifted uncomfortably in her seat but stayed quiet.

"She said, 'Ask your father. Oh God, he is going to have a stroke! And then she started laughing and called my Auntie and told her what I said.'"

Shea's mom shrugged, guilty of giggling at her daughter and not wanting to face the truth and talk about many parents' biggest fear—their child is most likely going to have sex at some time in his or her life.

The incident was funny, absolutely. It is giggle-worthy when your child says something that shocks and embarrasses you, but we don't want to humiliate our kids when they have questions about sex. Instead, it's important to take the opportunity to educate them so they know how to protect themselves. If you are going to get all giggly and embarrassed about talking with your daughter about sex, do it before you chat with her. If you don't think you can talk with her about sex without having a stroke, find someone who can!

Action 1: Get your giggles out before you have the sex talk with your daughter, or find a less giggly, but trustworthy and knowledgeable person to have the talk with her.

Having the sex talk does not mean that you are okay with your child having sex; it only means that you want to educate your child about sex to protect her. So if that is a fear of yours, get rid of it! Kids are curious about sex very early on, but that doesn't mean they are going to run out and have it just because they know about it. But if they do decide to have it, wouldn't you rather they knew how to protect themselves from diseases and pregnancy? These are scary things to think about, but they are necessary to address with your daughter. The sex talk isn't about scaring your kids out of having sex. It is about making sure that they understand what sex is, what to expect, how to protect themselves, and where to find answers to their questions.

What does the sex talk entail? There are certain topics that are very important to address with your daughter, and others that you may want to address only if she asks you about them. If you don't address topics you are too embarrassed to discuss, this will almost guarantee that your daughter will ask about these topics. It is almost as though they know exactly how to make you as uncomfortable as possible. For your sake, it is very important to plan out where you want to have the conversation, what you want to address in the conversation, and how to answer questions you find mortifying (without appearing mortified!).

When and where should you have the talk? If you put too much planning into when and where you have the sex talk, this is going to be totally obvious and probably make the sex talk even more awkward than it might otherwise have been. So try to pick a place that is private, and away from any older or younger siblings who could make the experience more embarrassing (this also includes partners who have not gotten their giggles out or who might be likely to tease your daughter). The car is always a great place for a talk; your daughter can completely avoid eye contact—and so can you! You might not get to choose the place because your daughter might choose it first. If you pick her up from school and she asks you what it means to "go down on someone," she has initiated the sex talk. There is no time like the present to continue. If she initiates the talk in a place that is less than ideal, however, either ask other family members to give you and your daughter privacy, or move to a space that is private.

Action 2: Figure out when to have the talk.

When do you have the talk? Sometimes, the talk happens because the school sends a letter home that informs you that sex education will be starting. In other instances, the talk may happen because your daughter asks a question about sex. Alternatively, you may simply decide that your daughter is ready for the talk. There is no magic age at which to have the talk. Eleven might be the perfect age for your daughter, while nine might be the perfect age for your niece. The right age for the talk will depend upon your daughter's maturity level and her level of curiosity. If she is immature, and one of the later bloomers in her class, you might have to bring up the topic before she is really interested in hearing about it. Waiting too long won't do her any good and will keep her behind her peers in terms of maturity. If you are afraid that the talk will mortify her, one good way of introducing the subject is to leave a book or two about sex in her room and then ask her if she has any questions about the book or books. This may also be helpful if you are mortified about bringing the topic up.

More often than not, the sex talk is broken up into different conversations that occur over a period of time. While you may have to initiate the first conversation, there are often conversations that follow, and that should follow. You want to be sure that when your daughter does have a question, you are there to answer it without making her feel ashamed about asking. The example at the beginning of the chapter is a good example of how mom missed a great opportunity to discuss sex with her daughter. Instead, she laughed at her and put her in another potentially embarrassing situation by recommending that she direct her question to her father. The more open you are about answering the questions your daughter has about sex, the more likely she is to ask you her questions. You do want her to feel comfortable about asking you questions!! So take advantage of opportunities when they are offered. You don't have to have an extensive conversation with her every time she asks a question. However, you can encourage her questions by concluding your answer with a statement such as, "Are there any other questions on your mind? I hope you know that you can always come to me with your questions."

Action 3: Recognize that there might not be one big sex talk that occurs. Instead, you may have a series of conversations with her about sex that unfold over time.

What should I discuss? What you discuss with her will depend a lot on her age and maturity. Although you might find the whole situation rather embarrassing, you can probably tell if any particular topic is an appropriate topic to address or not. Remember, you have a lot of control here over what you discuss, and how you discuss it. For example, if your four-year-old wants to know what a boner is, you could simply answer, "Something that happens to boys. Where did you hear that word?" A four-year-old doesn't need to know the answer or the details. It also would be important to know where she heard that word. Is there an older sibling who put her up to asking the question? Did she overhear something? As a parent, it is necessary to know these things. On the other hand, if your ten-year-old daughter asks what a boner is, you can tell her, "It is a slang term for an erection. Do you know what an erection is?" This will answer her question, and pave the way for more questions if necessary. You could ask her where she heard the word, but this may cause her to shut down a bit. It wouldn't be odd for kids her age to be talking about boners or giggling about various body parts and their nicknames.

There are different levels of the sex talk. For younger girls, the conversation may be focused around periods and why girls get them. This brings up sex in a very clinical way and can get the logistics of sex out there. A couple of years later, the sex talk may be revisited in the context of a conversation about your daughter's relationship seeming hot and heavy and a need to address birth control, sexually transmitted diseases, and pregnancy.

Action 4: Take care in matching the maturity level of your content to your daughter.

No matter when you have the sex talk, one important thing to keep in mind is that it should not be all negative. If sex was all negative, we wouldn't have to worry about our girls having it, and it wouldn't be an issue. Sex is not all negative, so don't pretend that it is. If you discuss sex as a completely negative act and associate it with girls who are provocative, get sexually transmitted diseases, risk teen pregnancy, endure painful relationships, and so on, you are not going to open the lines of communication at all. If you are realistic about sex, however, you might get somewhere when it comes to your daughter feeling comfortable talking to you about it. Talk to her about your concerns. Is she ready to have sex? Will she protect herself? Will she wish she waited? Will she end up being hurt by a boy who is just looking for sex? Talk to her about the good stuff, too. Sex is great when the time is right and the person is right. Sex is called making love for a reason; it can make you feel very connected to your partner. That connection can be very powerful, but it is something to be saved for an already sturdy relationship—not something to use to save a dying relationship. Sex should feel good. Sex should be fun. It is not something that should cause shame.

Discussing both the positives and the negatives of sex is a great way to make your conversation realistic and to make you seem more approachable. Although you don't want your little girl to grow up and you certainly don't want to think about her having sex, she is going to grow up and she is going to have sex. Since this is the case, don't you want her to enjoy it and not be uncomfortable about it? So many women have issues with sex. Wouldn't it be nice to raise a girl who didn't? Being open and honest about sex will help your daughter to develop a healthy relationship with her own sexuality.

Action 5: Don't focus on the negatives and scare your daughter; let her in on the good parts of sex, too!

Part of developing a healthy outlook about sex is knowing when and how to say "no." This is really hard to teach without sounding preachy. There will come a time when it's healthy for her to say "yes." You want to help put her in a position where she knows what to say. In thinking about sex, we often think about a male and a female having sexual intercourse. There are many other types of sexual contact, however, that you should address if your conversation has reached the point of discussing intercourse. If your daughter tells you not to worry, she is not going to have sex, and you walk away thrilled, turn around and find out what she considers sex and exactly what she is declining. You don't need details, but what you do need to know is what she considers sex? Is vaginal intercourse a "no," but anal sex a "yes"? Is oral sex a given? Does she date girls and therefore sees herself as never having to worry about saying "yes" or "no" to sex? Sex can be between two people, three people, or more. It can be anal, oral, or vaginal. If your only concern is with vaginal intercourse between a male and a female because of the potential consequences, consider the following:

- The level of intimacy is pretty high if she is having any type of sex, and if she is having one type, another is bound to follow.

- Sexually transmitted diseases can be transmitted during anal sex, oral sex, and from one girl to another.

- She could regret saying "yes" to anal sex or oral sex just as much as she could regret saying "yes" to vaginal intercourse.

So before you focus on sex as that which occurs between a male and a female, reconsider your approach. Think about all of her potential sexual activity. What are her morals? What does she think is too far too soon? Has she even thought about what she thinks of as sex? When you talk to her about morals, do so with curiosity— not with anger or suspicion. This is an interesting conversation to have, and you might get answers, but you will hopefully at least get her thinking about what might be too far for her, and where she is comfortable drawing the line. Once she knows her own comfort level with sex, she can then work on how to stick by her guns.

Action 6: Discuss what sex means to her, and have a conversation with her about morals.

Now that you and your daughter have figured out that there are all sorts of ways to have sex, work with her on ways of saying "no." This can be kind of fun and cheesy in an after-school special type of way. Just mentioning some of the old-school ways to say "no" might take the edge off the conversation. For example, "No life jacket, no swimming!" or "No party hat, no party!" Those are more geared toward wearing condoms, but if you can come up with some goofy ways of saying "no" or "slow down," you can then discuss more serious ways of saying "no," and equip your daughter with some options to draw from in the heat of the moment.

Here are a few things to let her know:

- She has control over her body, which is hers and no one else's. If she doesn't want something happening to it, she needs to protect it and say "no."

- If she is nervous that things might go too far, she should avoid putting herself in situations where it might be difficult to say "no." For example, she doesn't have to go to her boyfriend's unsupervised basement if she is afraid she will face the challenge of saying "no." She can say "no" by saying no to going down to the basement and instead suggest going to a movie or hanging out with other friends.

- If her date is getting too pushy sexually, she can call you. Let her know that she can call you from a date to be picked up—no questions asked. Pick her up and ask her if she is okay. Ask her if she wants to talk. Respect her answers. She was smart enough to call you and get help, so be happy that she felt comfortable calling you. If there was more to tell, she would probably tell you.

- If she is afraid someone will break up with her or not like her because she is not willing to do certain sexual things, then this person doesn't truly respect her and certainly is not worthy of her time or her intimacy.

After telling her these tips, let her know how wonderful she is and that she should never, ever, ever feel as though she *should* have sex with someone or that someone deserves to have sex with her just because he treated her well.

Action 7: Educate her on ways to say "no."

Now that she knows how and when to say yes or no, make sure she knows how to protect herself from sexually transmitted diseases (STDs) and unwanted pregnancy. There are new types of condoms and birth control coming out all the time, so do consult with a medical professional about the options. Take her to her primary care doctor or call your primary care doctor's office to find out about confidential teen clinics or family planning counselors who might be available to discuss birth control options with her, as well as how to best protect herself from STDs.

Many parents struggle with this as it seems permissive in that if you provide birth control, you are giving her the go-ahead as far as sex goes. This is not true. If she has decided she is going to have sex and you think the only thing stopping her is you not allowing her to go on the birth control pill, you are very naive. She will find a way to get birth control without you knowing or have sex without it. If you are totally against her having sex, it isn't a conversation about birth control that you need to be having. You need to instead discuss the importance of waiting. She might agree with you, or she might not agree with you. But don't get angry and take it out on her by not giving her access to birth control. It is better to have a daughter who had sex too soon with protection than a daughter who had sex too soon and ended up with herpes and an unwanted pregnancy.

Action 8: Find a health professional she can talk to about and access birth control.

What happens if you find out your daughter is having sex? Should you yell at her? Try to prevent her from ever seeing her boyfriend again? Lecture her on how she ruined her life? Punish her? No, no, no, no, no! Step outside and take a deep breath of fresh air. Don't freak out or even consider talking to her about it when you are overly emotional. Let the news sink in, then think about talking to her. First, are you sure, or are you jumping to conclusions? Make sure your source is reliable. How did you find out? Were you snooping? Did you find something? Did she tell you? How you found out is actually quite important. If you were snooping, then you have to come clean if you are going to confront her. If she told you, you are going to have to make sure that you don't have some horrible, knee-jerk reaction. If you found sexual paraphernalia like condoms or birth control pills, that isn't necessarily proof that the deed has been done, but is instead just proof that she is thinking about it and thinking about how to protect herself (smart girl).

Consider your emotions. Are you freaking out? Are you okay? Are you actually not all that surprised? If you are freaking out, why are you? Are you angry with her for doing something you don't think she should have done? Are you sad because you feel like she is growing up? Are you embarrassed because you are afraid that others will find out? Whatever the case, these are your emotions. You need to deal with them, not hurl them out at your daughter. What your daughter needs to see is that even though she has had sex, she is still your little girl. Sex is an act. Sure, in some ways, it means she is growing up because she is experiencing something new, but she is still the same girl. Sex doesn't change her DNA; it doesn't make her a different person. It is something she has now experienced, but it does not change the fact that she is your daughter, with all the same attributes as before. Think about your emotions and how they might be flavoring your reactions. If you are angry, could your anger come across as disgust? If you are sad, could your sadness come across as disappointment? If you are embarrassed, could your embarrassment come across as shame? You need to take care of these emotions before you react. Otherwise, your daughter could associate your negative emotions with her sexual experiences.

So what should you do? Now that you have taken a breather, remind yourself that sex doesn't change who your daughter is or the fact that she is your daughter. Hug her. Treat her the same way that you have always treated her. Ask her if she needs to talk? If you

decide you want to talk to her about sex, do so in a nonconfronta-
tional way.

What *not* to say:

- ☑ Oh my God, I can't believe you did this.
- ☑ What were you thinking????
- ☑ How many people have you had sex with?
- ☑ How many times have you guys had sex?
- ☑ I can't even look at you.
- ☑ Don't ever tell your father.
- ☑ Wait until your father finds out!
- ☑ What do you want, to get pregnant or something?
- ☑ You are never seeing him again!

What *to* say:

- ☑ Do you want to talk about it?
- ☑ It is going to take a little time for this to sink in, but only because it is scary for me to realize that you are growing up.
- ☑ I love you.
- ☑ Do you want to go to the health center to talk about birth control?
- ☑ Were you pressured in any way, or is there anything I should be worried about?
- ☑ Do you know you can always talk to me if you are ever worried about being pregnant or having an STD or anything?

Open the conversation up by letting her know that you aren't judging her and that you still love her. You want her to know that you are there for her and will continue to be there for her even though she has now had sex. It is important to acknowledge that this is a big step in her life, but also that she is still your little girl and you love her just the same. It is important to check in and just make sure that she was okay with having sex. You don't need to know the details, but you do need to know if she was pressured in any way.

Action 9: If you find out your daughter has had sex, you are going to go through a range of emotions, but try and keep your love for her as the primary focus. When all is said and done, love her and be there for her.

The three of them sat next to one another, Mom with her arms crossed, Dad with hands clasped together, and Kari with her knees hugged to her chest. They would not make eye contact.

Mom angrily said, "How can we not press charges?! How is this *her* decision? Her decision to go out with that jerk was obviously a bad one. How is it that we should let her decide whether or not she should pursue legal action?"

Kari put her head in her hands and sobbed. Dad put one hand on Kari's knee, and held up the other as if to stop Mom from speaking.

"We have to listen to her. She said she just wants to let it go. She isn't seeing him anymore, you already talked, or should I say *screamed* at his poor mother. I think we have done enough. Kari has to deal with all of this in a totally different way. She will be in all of his classes for the rest of the year. They have the same group of friends. She knows what she can handle."

Kari's body weight shifted toward Dad and her shoulders visibly relaxed. The sobbing slowed and everyone seemed to take a deep breath.

It is hard to know how you would react or how you would handle things if you found out your daughter was pressured into having sex. Many parents want to make the person who pressured their daughter pay in one way or another—by pursuing legal action, by threatening or physically hurting the person, or even by starting a smear campaign around town. While this is all understandable, the most important thing to do is to consider how your daughter feels about the situation and if she is ready or up to taking any action. This is definitely a situation that is generally dealt with well in counseling. Your daughter may want to do something about it, or she might not, but trying to work that out with parents who are so emotionally invested in her can be really difficult and bring with it a great deal of pressure. If she can talk to a neutral party such as a counselor about her situation, she will probably have an easier time working it out and recognizing what is best for her instead of making decisions based on what she thinks others want her to do. So before running over to this boy's house, let your daughter have some space to work things out in her own head. Don't talk about how awful he is every day. Talk about how much you love her every day and want her to be at peace with her decision.

If your daughter was forcibly taken advantage of or raped, it is important to link her with crisis counselors, the appropriate medical personnel, and a safe space. It is still important to give her time in decision making, but medical attention is imperative to assure she is okay.

Action 10: If you find out she was pressured into sex, listen to what she wants to do about the situation and give her the space to work it out with a neutral party.

What if your daughter confides in you that she thinks she did go too far too soon? How do you help her stick to her guns now? It can be a lot more difficult to say "no" once you have already said "yes."

Encourage her to take ownership of her body and talk to her about how to say "No, I don't want to, thank you very much." Changing her tune is tougher than sticking with a "no" or a "yes." Her partner may have expectations that sex is part of their relationship. She will have to talk to him about her thoughts and practice sticking to her guns.

Action 11: If she feels she went too far too soon, help her learn to say "no."

Sex may be one of the tougher issues because parents don't want to see their children as sexual beings. You don't need to think of her that way though; to you, she is the same girl she used to be— regardless of whether or not she has had sex!

Still wondering if you really need to have the talk? Here are some examples of questions and statements from teenagers regarding sex:

- ☑ If I use three condoms, am I better protected?

- ☑ As long as he pulls out early, I can't get pregnant.

- ☑ Oral sex isn't sex.

- ☑ I didn't want to have sex, but I didn't know what to say.

- ☑ If my boyfriend drinks lots of milk, will he have more sperm?

- ☑ If it is chocolate milk, will it taste better?

- ☑ As long as I pee right after, I won't get pregnant, right?

- ☑ My boyfriend says we should have sex because we have been together for six months, but I don't want to yet.

Chapter 7:
Action Recap

Action 1: Get your giggles out before you have the sex talk with your daughter, or find a less giggly, but trustworthy and knowledgeable person to have the talk with her.

Action 2: Figure out when to have the talk.

Action 3: Recognize that there might not be one big sex talk that occurs. Instead, you may have a series of conversations with her about sex that unfold over time.

Action 4: Take care in matching the maturity level of your content to your daughter.

Action 5: Don't focus on the negative and scare your daughter; let her in on the good parts of sex, too!

Action 6: Discuss what sex means to her, and have a conversation with her about morals.

Action 7: Educate her on ways to say "no."

Action 8: Find a health professional she can talk to about and access birth control.

Action 9: If you find out your daughter has had sex, you are going to go through a range of emotions, but try and keep your love for her as the primary focus. When all is said and done, love her and be there for her.

Action 10: If you find out she was pressured into sex, listen to what she wants to do about the situation and give her the space to work it out with a neutral party.

Action 11: If she feels she went too far too soon, help her learn to say "no."

Chapter 7:
Top Five Talking Points

1. Sex is a normal, natural, hopefully wonderful experience that you will have one day.

2. It is important for you to consider how ready you are for sex because once you have it, you can't take it back.

3. Consider what your morals are and stick to them!

4. Do you want to make an appointment to talk to your primary care doctor about sex and birth control? I thought you might want to talk to her instead of me. She knows more about birth control pills that are out there than I do.

5. I love you and I will continue to love you regardless of what decision you make about sex.

Chapter 7: *Resources*

http://www.sexetc.org/

For teens, by teens, but very useful for parents to get an idea of what kids really are going through at this age.

http://www.oprah.com/showinfo/How-to-Talk-to-Your-Kids-About
-Sex-with-Dr-Laura-Berman

Lengthy web address—awesome info. There is a step-by-step guide you can follow for having the sex talk, and tons of resources. Dr. Laura Berman is pretty cool and helpful.

http://www.aacap.org/cs/root/facts_for_families/talking_to_your_kids
_about_sex

The American Academy of Child and Adolescent Psychiatry has great information on how to talk to kids on tons of topics, and sex is one of them. It is pretty cut-and-dried information. Not a lot of fun stuff, but good information.

http://www.plannedparenthood.org/parents/how-talk-your-child
-about-sex-4422.htm

Planned Parenthood also has more information than just how to talk to your child about sex, but this section is very helpful.

EIGHT

Pregnancy and STDs— The Side Effects of Sex

Pregnancy and STDs make the fact that your daughter has had sex quite the reality, and now other people will need to be involved and discuss your daughter's sexual activity, which can be tough on both you and your daughter.

PREGNANCY

The nurse went into the waiting room to get Cindy's mom. Cindy's mom knew right away that something was wrong. "What is it?"

"Well, she has something to tell you." The nurse led her into the exam room where Cindy sat, her face covered in tears. Cindy looked at the nurse desperately.

The nurse sighed and looked at Mom, "Cindy is pregnant. I will leave you two to talk."

Cindy sobbed uncontrollably.

Reaction One:

Mom bursts into tears, too. "I can't believe this! Your father is going to kill you! How could you do this?!!"

Reaction Two:

Mom walks over and slaps Cindy across the face. "What did I tell you about sex? Not until after marriage. Good luck finding somewhere to live."

Reaction Three:

Mom walks over to Cindy and wraps her arms around her. "We'll figure this out, sweetie. It will be okay. I love you very much and we will get through this together."

In the moment, the mother probably wants the floor to swallow her, but her initial response will affect how the rest of the journey plays out. Regardless of what she says, she might turn out to be incredibly supportive after she thinks it through and realizes that her daughter needs her to be strong, but her initial reaction does have an impact.

But what if the mom is scared, horrified, or livid? What should she do in the moment? This is one of those times where she ought to feel that she can lie to her child without having to feel guilty. She should either say nothing except the words "I love you," or, if she says more, she may need to lie about how she is feeling. She may have to swallow her anger and replace it with, "Don't worry, honey. Everything will be okay." Even though her emotions may be all over the place, she may need to stick them in a cubby somewhere in her head and recognize that her baby needs her unconditional love right now. The chances are good that her daughter is worried about all the same things that are worrying her mom. She may be thinking about such things as:

What am I going to do? How do I tell my boyfriend? His parents are going to be so angry. What will happen with school? How do I decide what is best for me? She probably also has begun to realize that, no matter what she decides, her life has changed forever.

Congratulations to those parents who have a calm and loving reaction under the circumstances. But for those parents who flipped out, all is not lost! These parents do need, however, to gather themselves as quickly as possible so that they can help their daughter. The first step to take is to tell your daughter you love her. Apologize for the not very thoughtful initial response, whatever it was. Tell her the news took you by surprise and you reacted too quickly, but that what matters most is that you love her and will be there for her.

Action 1: Let her know that you love her.

Wrap your arms around your daughter, and let her know that you will help her with her decision, and through this time. Let her know that she will be okay. There is no need for a decision to be made instantly, at a time of overwhelming emotions. Even if she knows without a doubt what she wants to do, it won't hurt to wait twenty-four hours to revisit the issue and sit with it. If she decides to terminate the pregnancy, a doctor can advise her about the procedures and timing required.

Action 2: You and your daughter need to take time to clear your heads.

While you may be tempted to talk to your sister, mother, or a best friend, because so much is at stake and because confidentiality is important, involving professionals is really a wise course at this time. She should see a doctor, who can examine her, monitor her condition, and advise her regarding her options. She also may wish to see a counselor, who can help provide the emotional support she probably needs at this time. No matter what decision she makes, this is not going to be an easy time. She will have to live with whatever decision she makes for the rest of her life. Resources can be found through your doctor's office or by contacting a local Planned Parenthood chapter, or a free clinic in your area. There are quite a few teen clinics across the country, and it is often the teens, school nurses, and local health centers that know where they are. This might be a more comfortable option for both you and your daughter if you are anxious about confidentiality.

Action 3: Talk to someone who can help medically and emotionally.

Will talking to family or friends about this really benefit anyone? People tend to have very strong emotions regarding intimacy and pregnancy. They may not reveal their true feelings upfront, and you may not know their own history with intimacy and pregnancy. If your daughter chooses to have the baby, you will eventually have to tell people what is happening. If she decides to give the baby up for adoption, the last thing she needs is someone making judgments or putting their two cents in about the decision. Wait until she is 100 percent confident about her decision and until she is ready for others to know. If she is going to terminate, does anyone really need to know? Her grandmother may treat her differently because she knows, an aunt may make a snide remark, or a cousin may spread the news around the family; none of these things will be helpful for her. If at all possible, avoid such judgments and the possibility of rumors being spread.

Your daughter may be eager to confide in her best friend. Unfortunately, her best friend at the age of twelve may be her enemy at the age of fourteen, and she could really use this information to hurt your daughter. Encourage her to keep this information private and to discuss it with a counselor, not her clique.

Action 4: Zip your lips.

Once the decision is made, let it settle. Your daughter will need some time after her decision is made to sit with her feelings. She is going to feel uneasy. No matter how awesome you have been, she may wonder if you really will be there for her, or if you will turn on her. She may feel pretty self-conscious around you for a while, especially if you are the only person who knows about her pregnancy. Even after months have passed, your daughter may seem very sensitive when you become angry with her. If she is feeling not so great about herself, she could come across as excessively needy. Watch out for these reactions, and try as hard as possible to keep communications open with her about any anxiety or depression she may be feeling. You might need to provide her with extra love and support during this period. There may be times when she seems fine, which may be followed by a day when she feels down in the dumps. Be there for her to lean on, and if it seems like things are not getting any better for her, take action by finding her a support group or a counselor.

Action 5: Continue to actively support and love your daughter.

How do you learn to trust her again? Will you worry when she goes out with her boyfriend? Will your anxiety level rise if her period seems irregular? Probably. One thing that might help you a bit and help her a great deal, would be to talk to her about sex and birth control all over again. Revisit these issues, and make sure she is protected and that she understands she could get pregnant again or get a disease. Don't approach these topics in a scary way, like "You'd better not get pregnant again!" Instead, try something along the lines of, "That was a really tough experience for you. I just don't want to see it happen again, and there are a lot of ways to protect yourself against it happening again." Much nicer!

Action 6: Revisit the sex and birth control talk.

SEXUALLY TRANSMITTED DISEASES (STDS)

For some reason, people seem to have compassion for a girl who gets pregnant, but look at a girl who gets an STD as dirty in some way. There is an unfortunate assumption that having an STD means a person is promiscuous. This could be, but your daughter can get infected with an STD the first time she has sex. If her partner has one, she is likely to get one. She could have sex with someone who has three STDs and end up getting all three of them. Is she promiscuous? No. She just happened to have sex with someone who has STDs. Try and take the idea that she is sleeping around out of it. Just like with pregnancy, you need to love her, support her, get her medical help and hopefully counseling, keep it private, continue to support her even after she is treated, and revisit the sex and protection talk.

Action 7: Try and take the stigma and shame away from her diagnosis.

Of course, there are some STDs that are not curable and make life as a young person very difficult. Some of the noncurable STDs are:

- ☑ **Human Papilloma Virus (HPV)**—This virus causes genital warts and some strains cause cervical cancer. There is a vaccine for it that can protect your daughter from some of the more dangerous strains of this virus, but not all of them. It is important to talk to her healthcare provider about the benefits and risks of this vaccine.

- ☑ **Herpes**—This virus can be transmitted orally as well. There are treatments for the symptoms, but no cure.

☑ **Hepatitis C**—This can be transmitted sexually, but is most often seen in folks who have had contact with IV drugs or who have had a partner who used IV drugs and had hepatitis C.

☑ **HIV**—This is still out there and it is still not curable.

All of these can be managed, but when it comes down to it, once you have it you have it, and you can give it to others. Your daughter will need to learn that she must be up front with any current or future partners about her sexual history so that these partners know that they are at risk for contracting the disease. Be sure you help her find the education and support she needs to protect herself and her partner or partners in the future.

Action 8: Educate yourself and your daughter about her STD and make sure she knows how to talk to her future partner or partners about the situation.

Chapter 8:
Action Recap

PREGNANCY

Action 1: Let her know that you love her.

Action 2: You and your daughter need to take time to clear your heads.

Action 3: Talk to someone who can help medically and emotionally.

Action 4: Zip your lips.

Action 5: Continue to actively support and love your daughter.

Action 6: Revisit the sex and birth control talk.

STDS

Action 1: Let her know that you love her.

Action 2: You and your daughter need to take time to clear your head.

Action 3: Talk to someone who can help medically and emotionally.

Action 4: Zip your lips.

Action 5: Continue to actively support and love your daughter.

Action 6: Revisit the sex and birth control talk.

Action 7: Try and take the stigma and shame away from her diagnosis.

Action 8: Educate yourself and your daughter on her STD and make sure she knows how to talk to future partners about the situation.

Chapter 8:
Top Five Talking Points

1. I love you.

2. We will get through this together.

3. This is heavy stuff; seeing a doctor is critical and talking to a counselor could also be really helpful.

4. Be careful who you talk to about this; keeping it private might be best.

5. The next time you are thinking about having sex, I hope you use all of this knowledge you have to protect yourself and your partner. You have control over your sex life.

Chapter 8: *Resources*

http://www.sexetc.org/

This website is geared toward teens, so it wouldn't be appropriate for some of the younger girls, but it does contain great information.

http://answer.rutgers.edu/

This site is the parent site of www.sexetc.org and provides great resources for parents and other professionals on sexual health.

http://www.plannedparenthood.org/

This site has listings of confidential clinics and tons of resources.

NINE

Learning Disabilities

When Alexis was nine years old, she started to really struggle in school. Instead of receiving comments like, "Alexis is a pleasure to have in class," Alexis now brought home below-average grades and comments like, "Alexis is talking excessively" or "Alexis is having difficulty staying on task." One of her teachers recommended that she be evaluated for a learning disability. This recommendation made Alexis's mom quite angry.

"Do they think my daughter has lost brain cells overnight? She isn't dumb. There is nothing wrong with her. The problem must be her teacher. I heard from another parent that the teacher did the same thing to her daughter, and her daughter turned out to be fine. Now Alexis is so upset about her grades that she doesn't even want to go to school. It is almost impossible to get her out of bed in the morning. Then I spend the rest of the morning yelling at her to hurry up and get to school!"

"Have you had Alexis evaluated for a learning disability?"

"No! My daughter is not stupid."

Alexis, sitting silently in the corner, bursts into tears.

"Don't worry, Alexis. I know you aren't dumb. You don't need special classes. You just need a teacher who can do her job."

Let's stop here. What is up with Alexis's mother? Does she care about Alexis? Without a doubt. Is she someone who will advocate for Alexis? Absolutely. Does she think Alexis is smart? Yes. Is Alexis's education important to her? Completely.

What about Alexis? She hasn't said a peep. Is something going on with her? Probably. She is sometimes refusing to go to school and her grades have been declining. She is anxious and upset. She could be experiencing something totally unrelated to school. Perhaps Alexis's teacher is not very good at her job. Alexis could be more interested in socializing than in doing schoolwork. But perhaps Alexis does have a learning disability.

If you were Alexis and you just heard your mom rattling on, how would you feel? You would probably be pretty worried about the possibility of being diagnosed with a learning disability, which in her mother's mind apparently means being stupid. But having a learning disability most certainly does not mean that the person who has it is stupid.

A learning disability, as defined by LD Online, is "a neurological disorder. In simple terms, a learning disability results from a difference in the way a person's brain is 'wired.' Children with learning disabilities are as smart or smarter than their peers. But they may have difficulty reading, writing, spelling, reasoning, recalling and/or organizing information if left to figure things out by themselves or if taught in conventional ways."

Action 1: Understand the meaning of a learning disability.

Now that you know what a learning disability is, do you think Alexis or her mom fully understand the definition of a learning disability? It doesn't seem as though they do. It seems as though Alexis's mom thinks that the teacher is implying that Alexis can't do the work that is assigned to her, when in reality, the teacher might be thinking that the way Alexis learns could be better catered to in a class with different teaching methods, or even in her current class— with some adjustments to how things are presented to Alexis. But Alexis is hearing that having a learning disability will mean that she is stupid and a disappointment to her Mom. As a parent, you must be really careful how you react to unexpected news about your child. Whether it is a medical, educational, or even a mental health issue, if you even remotely imply that this issue would mean that your child is a disappointment to you, this is what she will remember. We don't know what the future holds for our children, so we may sometimes be surprised or even disappointed by unexpected developments. It is important, however, to keep in mind how your reaction could impact your child in a negative way. Alexis isn't even diagnosed with a learning disability, yet she is already worried that if she is diagnosed with one, she will be letting her mom down.

Action 2: Keep in mind how your reactions to potentially disappointing news can affect your daughter.

Upon meeting with Alexis alone, it was clear that she was having difficulties with school, but she had been afraid to let her Mom know how much she was struggling.

"It isn't like I don't try, but lately school just seems so hard that I would rather not go. I could always do my work before, but I would spend a long time doing it. Now I feel like I am too confused to really get any of it done. I feel like I read but nothing sinks in. Then when the teacher asks questions about the reading, I can't remember anything. My friends laugh at me, and I don't feel comfortable going to school. When I ask my mom for help, she just says, 'Oh Alexis, you know how to do that.' And I do know how to do it, but I can't seem to get it done. Am I stupid? *Did* something happen to my brain cells?"

Alexis tried to tell her mom about her struggles, but Mom basically ignored them. Because Alexis wasn't getting the help she needed, she was feeling overwhelmed, anxious, frustrated, and ashamed. To make matters worse, her friends weren't being supportive. Not only was her learning disability making it hard for her to learn, but also, she was feeling a lot of stress, and stress makes any type of learning more difficult.

What could Mom have done differently to help Alexis? Her reaction to the teacher's concerns could have been much more calming for Alexis. Instead of claiming the teacher was an idiot, Mom could have asked the teacher why she thought Alexis should be tested. If she had done this, she might have found out more about why the teacher was concerned about Alexis. If she wasn't so determined to prove that the teacher was wrong, she could have had a conversation with Alexis about why Alexis was struggling. Simply asking Alexis more about school and the work that she was doing may have given her more information on why Alexis might need to be tested for a learning disability.

With the appropriate information from school and from Alexis, Mom would be in a much better position to take some control over the situation and advocate for Alexis to receive any testing that could help make the picture clearer.

Action 3: Gather information from your daughter, her teachers, and any other persons with relevant information about your daughter's learning style and learning difficulties.

This seems easy enough, so why was Mom so judgmental at the outset? Often, as parents, we forget how many expectations we put on our children. Parents tend to hand the toy truck to their son, the Barbie to their daughter. Maybe your daughter wants the truck. Maybe she hates dolls. You sign her up for activities, and automatically sign her up for cheerleading and gymnastics. Maybe she would prefer to play football. You may talk about how great college was, and how you and your partner met while in a heated debate team competition. Maybe your daughter struggles with being able to think quickly. When she hears you talk about people with learning disabilities as dumb, she may assume that she will never be able to go to college. So be cautious about your expectations. Your daughter can be smart and successful even though she has a learning disability; however, her education might shape up somewhat differently than it would have if she didn't have one. Instead of being on the debate team, she might be on the chess team. Instead of getting straight As in all her academics, she might earn straight As in all her music classes. Your daughter may learn differently than other members of her family; she may need help in areas where her parents or siblings excel.

Hearing your child has a learning disability can also be quite scary. What does it mean for her? Will she have to go into special classes? Is college still a possibility? Some parents may need time to grieve in a sense because the expectations they have for their child may no longer seem realistic. But parents who can let go of their expectations and any sadness they may feel that things aren't the way that they had hoped can then open their eyes to new possibilities for their daughter. If every person's brain was wired in the conventional way, we would have a very boring world. So let go of your expectations. Take time to grieve if you must, then open your eyes to new possibilities. New possibilities can be scary, but they can also be truly exciting.

Action 4: Let go of your expectations and keep your mind open to new possibilities in learning and in life for your daughter.

Now that you have emotionally processed that your daughter could have a learning disability, it is time for action. It is time to have her tested, learn what the testing reveals about her, become as informed as possible about the results, advocate for her, help her understand what the results mean, and help her deal with any difficulties she may face in dealing with her learning disability.

Look at the information you gathered in Action 3. If there is any possibility that she has a learning disability, then have her tested. It is better to know so you can deal with the issue then to send her into a class that isn't meeting her needs. A school psychologist usually does the testing for a learning disability. To have your child tested, you must give the school *written* permission to do so. If you just call and ask for it, it doesn't have to happen. Once you ask in writing for the school to test your child, your child will go through a series of tests that vary depending on the school and the tester. Tests generally show your child's IQ, reveal any major discrepancies between your child's abilities in certain subject areas, and provide information on memory, decoding, processing speeds, and emotional well-being. The psychologist will often use personal observations and observations by teachers to create a report on your child. In the report, your child's results should be explained. The report should also say whether your child has a learning disability.

Action 5: If there is concern that your daughter may have a learning disability, take the necessary steps to find out if she does.

If it is discovered that your child does in fact have a learning disability, the school will then need to write an Individualized Education

Plan (IEP) within thirty days of determining that your child has a learning disability. An IEP is a legal document that lays out what a child needs to have in place to meet goals that the IEP team has planned for the child. The IEP team is made up of the person or persons who tested your child, someone who can interpret those results (most often this is the person who did the evaluation), a special education representative, a regular education teacher, a parent or guardian, and—when appropriate—the child. Sometimes, the parent also hires an outside consultant who attends the meeting as well. It is generally put together at a meeting of the team members, and includes the child's strengths, areas that need improvement, goals, accommodations to be put in place to meet these goals, and where the child best fits in terms of classes (will she be in resource classes, small classes, a different school setting, etc.). At the meeting, everyone has an opportunity to make suggestions on what sort of education will best suit the child. A consensus is reached, and the IEP is created. Once the IEP is written, you can still disagree with it and take further action such as having your child evaluated by an independent evaluator.

This is just a taste of the special education process. It can be really confusing and can feel very overwhelming. It may seem easiest to just sign whatever the professionals tell you to sign. Don't do that!!! It is important that parents understand what the testing means, what the child's disability is, and what the IEP is recommending. You are the advocate for your child. The goal is to get your child's needs met in the least restrictive environment, meaning your child should be in a small setting if and only if she needs a small setting, not because that is the only place they can fit her. If you read all the documents they provide, ask questions, and look into resources such as those at the end of this chapter, and still feel confused, you are not alone. It could be worthwhile to seek outside help even if it is just to help you figure out all the acronyms. Some states have educational advocates who work for free through state grants; some states do not have such resources. Ask other parents or relatives who have had experience with a child with a learning disability for recommendations on who to talk to for help. Don't be embarrassed or ashamed if you are confused. It can be very confusing, and it can seem even worse if you are feeling overwhelmed or anxious.

Action 6: Make sure you understand the meaning of the testing, your daughter's learning disability, and the IEP.

The emotional as well as practical aspects of learning disabilities can also be daunting. How do you talk to your daughter about her learning disability? What if her IEP puts her in a class that will separate her from her friends? What if her friends tease her? Is her learning disability significant enough that it could keep her from pursuing her dream of becoming a doctor? If you thought figuring out how to deal with a learning disability was confusing, imagine how confusing it is for your daughter.

First of all, how can you best explain her learning disability to her? Being direct can often work wonders. Simply explaining to her that her mind works a bit differently and that she needs a different type of teaching to learn might be all you need to do when she is younger. As she gets older, she will develop a greater understanding of how she learns best, what accommodations she needs to succeed, and why she needs them. If you hide the fact that she has a learning disability and tell her she is in "special classes" because she is "special," she is going to figure out the sugar coating one day and be pretty annoyed. She will also realize you are ashamed of her learning disability since you were taking steps to hide it. You are better off letting her know the truth. The details of her testing won't really make sense to her when she is eight, nine, ten, or even eleven, but as she gets older, she should start to develop (with your assistance) a better grasp of how the whole system works. She needs to learn to advocate for herself, and the only way she can become effective at this is if she understands what she needs to be successful in her classes.

It is important to remember that your daughter's learning disability, although potentially only glaringly obvious in school, is not just an in-school issue. Harriette Wimms, Ph.D, from Maryland's Mariposa Child Success Programs, points out that a learning disability affects learning in school as well as learning out of school. This makes it crucial for you as the parent to be a strong role model outside of school so your daughter can learn social cues and interactions by observing you. You are teaching your daughter with every action.

A great way for both a parent and daughter to understand her learning disability is to talk to a teacher who has had success in teaching her. Teachers can be great at simplifying what a child's learning disability entails. Your daughter's teacher can explain the ways in which a student struggles and what she needs to learn best. For example, a teacher who teaches Alexis might say, "Alexis seems to get really fidgety when we read for a long period of time in class. When I ask class members what they read, Alexis tries to get out of answering any questions. She often says that she can't remember what she read, or didn't understand it. When I sit one-on-one with Alexis and have her read one paragraph at a time and underline important points, Alexis can get all the way to the end of a section and answer questions. I think Alexis needs her work and directions broken down into smaller segments, help staying on task, more individualized attention, and positive reinforcement when she succeeds."

This teacher is basically saying that when Alexis is overwhelmed by too much work, she fidgets and becomes distracted. When the work is broken down and Alexis is shown how to pull out important points, then Alexis can focus better and stay on task. This could easily be explained to Alexis. She could then let future teachers know that she does better when work is broken down and when teachers help her to stay on task. Involve teachers in helping you and your daughter understand how your daughter learns best and when she struggles. That way, both of you will be better able to let others know the best ways in which to help her succeed. If your daughter can truly understand what she needs, she will be more successful in school and more likely to get the help she needs.

Action 7: Explain to your daughter what her learning disability means, what she needs to succeed, and the tools she needs to learn so that she can advocate for herself.

A resource room here or there, an inclusion class for math, an extra class on how to improve reading comprehension—these all sound relatively minimal in terms of special education changes. Sometimes, the changes are not that minimal, and you could see your daughter's entire schedule change so that she is in all special education classes, or receives a number of resource room classes. In any of these scenarios, your daughter could encounter teasing or a separation from her friends. She might feel as if she is different, but not in a good way. How can you help her deal with the emotional aspects of a learning disability?

You need to be there to answer her questions and concerns. A sampling of questions, concerns, and ideas for answers include:

- "Am I stupid? Frank said I go to the resource room because I am dumb."

"No! You are not stupid at all. You go to the resource room because you need extra help in math class. It is great that you go because going will help you get better math grades and understand math better. Your willingness to go shows that you are smart! Try to ignore Frank or anyone else who says anything like that. He is not being very kind."

- "I don't want to go to special education classes. They are stupid and all my friends are in my old classes."

  "I bet it is really tough to change all of your classes—especially since all of your friends are in the old ones. I am sorry you can't be in their classes. That really does stink. But you've got to at least give the new classes a try. Hopefully, they will help you to better understand the subjects—maybe that way, you won't get so frustrated with your homework and you will have more time after school to see your friends. You could also make friends in your new classes."

- "It is so embarrassing when Sheila, the speech therapist, comes to take me out of class. It causes all sorts of commotion, and everyone turns to look and asks where I am going."

  "Hmm. I'll bet that is kind of disruptive. Do you want me to talk to Sheila to see if she can get you right at the end of a class or if you can wait for her in the office after class so your class is not disrupted and you are not embarrassed?"

- "I know you are telling me I am not stupid, but I *feel* stupid. I can't read as fast as everyone, it takes me a lot longer to get my work done, and when I answer questions in class, it takes me a while to get my idea across."

"Well, I am going to continue to tell you that you aren't stupid because you aren't stupid. I can understand that it must be frustrating to deal with this issue. I know it is harder for you and that really isn't fair. I wish I could change that, but I can't. The important thing is that you are working hard and continuing to do the work even though it is really tough for you. Let's keep talking about how smart you should feel since you are smart and you are smart to be trying so hard!

Also, let's keep in mind that school is only one part of your life. You are more than just how fast you read. You are a great volleyball player, a fun friend, and amazing at photography. So, when you start to feel down about school, think about stuff that you love to do and that you do well!"

These are all questions that are likely to come up in some way, shape, or form. When you are answering questions like these, try to think about reinforcing that your daughter is *not stupid*. Learning disabilities do not equal stupid. It is really unfortunate that people think that way. Some ways that learning disabilities can make kids feel especially different include being pulled out by various providers or teachers for some sort of extra resource or therapy. Although it would be great if your daughter were not embarrassed when someone pulls her out of class, if she is embarrassed, there is nothing wrong with trying to coordinate with teachers and other school employees on other ways of connecting with your daughter so that she doesn't feel so obviously "different." Also, try to talk to your daughter about appreciating herself as a whole person, and not just about how she does in school. School right now is a huge part of her identity, but try and help her see beyond school and to get her to appreciate the other facets of her identity.

The dreaded repeating a grade . . . If the school suggests that your daughter repeat a grade, make sure that you weigh the positives and negatives. Find out if there are other options, such as summer school or tutoring? Repeating a grade can be helpful at times, but students who are retained are at greater risk of dropping out of school and that is certainly something to avoid. So just be sure to go over any possible alternatives and find out how repeating the grade will help your daughter. Talk to your daughter about it as well and see what her thoughts are on the subject. In some instances, such as when your daughter might be starting in a new school with a whole group of students or with very little overlapping of students from her prior school, repeating a grade can be a very successful intervention.

Action 8: Protect your daughter's self-esteem by reinforcing that she is more than just her success or difficulty in school.

As the school years pass, it may become apparent that college might not be the best option for your daughter or that becoming a doctor is unlikely. When these roadblocks come up, it is important to go back to the advice in the last section and think of your daughter as a whole person. She is more than just school and academics. She can be a great success and a great contributing member of society, even if she has a very significant learning disability. There is no reason why she cannot have success in her life. When thinking of her as a whole person, you might have to help her think outside the box and think about what she really loves to do.

If her heart is set on being a doctor or a lawyer or an FBI agent, but it is unlikely to happen, encourage her to explore other careers in those fields. There are plenty of really interesting professions in the medical field that do not require medical school or even college.

Help her find ways to be involved in the fields she enjoys at a level where she can achieve success.

Action 9: Help your daughter think outside the box and appreciate herself as more than just academics.

Special education is tricky and confusing. The laws are changing and the whole process can be overwhelming. Get support for yourself so you can advocate and teach your daughter to advocate for herself.

Chapter 9:
Action Recap

Action 1: Understand the meaning of a learning disability.

Action 2: Keep in mind how your reactions to potentially disappointing news can affect your daughter.

Action 3: Gather information from your daughter, her teachers, and any other person with relevant information about your daughter's learning style and learning difficulties.

Action 4: Let go of your expectations and keep your mind open to new possibilities in learning and in life for your daughter.

Action 5: If there is concern that your daughter may have a learning disability, take the necessary steps to find out if she does.

Action 6: Make sure you understand the meaning of the testing, your daughter's learning disability, and the IEP.

Action 7: Explain to your daughter what her learning disability means, what she needs to succeed, and the tools she needs to learn so that she can advocate for herself.

Action 8: Protect your daughter's self-esteem by reinforcing that she is more than just her success or difficulty in school.

Action 9: Help your daughter think outside the box and appreciate herself as more than just academics.

Chapter 9:
Top Five Talking Points

1. It seems like you are struggling a bit in school and that some of your teachers are concerned. They are suggesting that we have you tested to see if you might have a learning disability. I think it can't hurt to have the testing done, especially if the answers can help us. What do you think?

2. Having a learning disability is not your fault and it does not mean that you are stupid or dumb or not trying. It just means that you learn a bit differently.

3. It is important that you understand what you need to be effective in school. If you understand these things, you can make sure you get what you need from your teachers. If you don't feel like you are getting what you need, let me know.

4. When you think about yourself and who you are, remember that you are more than just your grades and school. You have other interests and you excel at all sorts of things. Don't let difficulties in one area get you down.

5. Is there anything you would like to do or that you would like me to do that would help you to learn better or to help you understand your learning disability better?

Chapter 9: *Resources*

http://www.ldonline.org/

This site has a great basics section that breaks everything down. It also defines the most common learning disabilities.

http://idea.ed.gov/

This site is important because it goes over IDEA 2004 and explains what IDEA (Individuals with Disabilities Education Act) is. It is also a bit overwhelming, though, so you might want to stick to the "major topics" area of the website. This website is still in the works and will continue to change as laws and policies change.

http://www.fape.org/idea/2004/summary.htm

This site is more user-friendly than the government one above and states the most important points of IDEA in a way that is understandable.

http://www.doe.mass.edu/sped/links/learndisability.html

This is the Massachusetts Department of Education's site for learning disabilities and has links for all the major specific learning disability sites. It is definitely helpful.

TEN

Mental Illness

This is a big, scary term. People hear the term "mental illness" and think "crazy." They associate the words "mental illness" with words like hallucinations, suicide, mania, schizophrenia, long term, incurable, hopeless, and overwhelming. Mental illness encompasses some severe illnesses, but it also includes illnesses such as adjustment disorder, which is a change in her life (moving, changing schools, parents divorcing, etc.) to which she has a hard time adjusting. Something like adjustment disorder doesn't sound very scary, right? So when you think of mental illness, and you read this chapter, try to keep an open mind. All disorders are treatable. Are they all curable? They are not always curable, but they are definitely manageable. There is help out there for every type of disorder. No matter what you think your child might have or does have, there is help for you, for her, and for your family. All you need to do is access that help.

If your daughter has not been diagnosed with anything, but you are concerned that she is suffering, please take her to see her primary care physician or another medical professional. Don't try and diagnose her on your own; don't let your family and friends tell you what they think she has. Take control over the situation and bring her to a healthcare professional who can, not only figure out what is going on with your daughter, but also can direct you to helpful counselors and services.

Keep in mind that girls go through quite a bit. Your daughter might not end up with a diagnosis. Instead, she could be going through a phase, or just need someone to talk to as her hormones run amuck. The best thing you can do for her, however, is to respond to your instincts that something is not right and get her some help.

Action 1: If you are concerned that your daughter may have a mental illness, take her to see her primary care physician or another health professional.

We are going to look at a scenario of a young lady with one type of disorder, but the actions to take are similar no matter what type of disorder you suspect. Because there are so many disorders with their own treatments and nuances, this chapter won't deal with the specifics but will take a general approach. We will talk about anxiety since this is so common among women. There are resources at the end of the chapter that should help you access the help you need for any sort of mental illness.

"I think it is the hand washing." Megan's father was distraught that his daughter had been uninvited to a party of her closest friends. Megan was diagnosed with obsessive compulsive disorder (OCD). At times, she would spend hours washing her hands. Her friends and even their parents felt that they could no longer manage her compulsions. Mom stopped attending family counseling sessions because she had grown so angry and frustrated with Megan that she felt her presence was making Megan more anxious and stressed out.

Mom vocalized her frustration in the last meeting she attended, "I just don't understand what to do. We bring her here, we have tried to take any stress at home away, we started that medicine, we do fun things with her, and she has us at her beck and call. What more can we do? This is taking up all of our time and, frankly, it is ruining our lives. Is that what you want to do, Megan? Make us all miserable? I have missed too many days at work. My family keeps telling me how they think I should handle it. I feel like a bad parent, and nothing is getting better! I am starting to think counseling only made it worse. Perhaps if we had just punished her for acting crazy, we would have gotten better results. Sometimes, it seems like she is just using this 'illness' to manipulate us. I think she just needs to suck it up and get over it already!"

Dad looked ill after Mom blurted all of this out. Megan looked upset, but not overly surprised, which suggested that she had heard her mother make these kinds of comments before. Dad tried to stick up for Megan, "Don't yell at her!! Who in their right mind would wash their hands all day? She even missed the school play because of it. Don't you feel bad for her? I know it has been a lot to handle, but what else can we do? I just have to believe that she will get better, and I wish you would believe it, too. I don't think *your* attitude is very helpful."

Let's break this up a bit to see what is going on and how we can manage it better. Megan has a serious mental illness that is not only affecting her but is also impacting her social relationships and her family. Mom has been trying to help. However, she is frustrated with Megan, having a hard time understanding why Megan can't just get better, anxious about her job, questioning her own ability as a parent, upset about the impact the illness has on the family, wondering if Megan is just manipulating everyone, and feeling as though nothing is working. Dad comes across as the caring one. He feels badly for Megan, and he seems frustrated with Mom for not showing more compassion. Who is right? Is Megan being manipulative? Is Dad being too nice? Is Mom really mean? Maybe yes. Maybe no. Mental illness can be really tough to deal with for everyone involved. If we look closely, we may be able to shed light on each person's reaction and to help each person learn to react in a way that is more helpful to Megan.

One thing parents everywhere need to learn is that they cannot control their child's mental illness. They cannot control how severe it is, or how long it will take to see improvement. They can learn to provide the best and most supportive environment for their child, but unfortunately it is not likely that they can just make it disappear. Some mental illnesses are short-lived, and not chronic, while others can be chronic and unpredictable. It is important to recognize what you cannot control and to learn to work with it as best as you can.

Action 2: Understand that you cannot control your child's mental illness. But you can do your best to provide a supportive environment for your child.

When adults feel that they are losing control, they tend to act in one of two ways. They either ignore the problem or they get really angry; neither one of these tactics work very well in the long run. Initially, both reactions may appear to help. When you ignore the problem, you feel better because you think that you have come up with a solution. Your daughter may stop telling you when she is feeling badly or upset because you aren't listening. For a period of time, it may seem as though the problem has gone away. This never lasts, though; eventually, if your daughter needs help, she will do whatever she needs to do to get you to pay attention. The angry reaction gets similar results. When you are angry, you feel like you are being pro-active, and your emotions have somewhere to go. But if you are angry, your daughter will probably be too scared to tell you that she is not doing well; you may think that she is doing better, when in reality, she may just be hiding her feelings.

If these reactions make you feel better for a while, what is the harm? Well, for one thing, your daughter might actually be getting worse. She might start hiding how she is really feeling from you. She could be spiraling down pretty quickly, and you might not realize it until it becomes a crisis. Megan might be telling her mom that she didn't wash her hands all day; isn't that great? In reality, she may be sneaking places to wash her hands, or feeling so stressed about washing her hands that she turns to unhealthier methods of stress relief. The other way she may react is to ramp up the urgency of her illness. Her symptoms might get worse to the point where you must pay attention or you can no longer be angry because she is now in real danger. Megan could lock herself in the bathroom and not come out or let anyone else in until an adult helps her. The goal is to avoid any unnecessary drastic measures by remaining as open and as calm as possible about the situation. Will this prevent your daughter from turning to unhealthy coping mechanisms? Not always, but hopefully it will help her feel supported enough that she won't have to resort to unhealthy measures.

What if you read this and think, "Great. Now I am totally invalidated and I am supposed to suppress my own anger." No! That is not what I am suggesting. You can be angry; you can want to bury your head in the sand. But you can't be angry with your daughter about her illness, and you can only bury your head in the sand for a short period. Be angry at the illness. Throw yourself into your running routine every day and zone out for an hour. Find ways to cope with your anxiety, anger, and fear. Face the fact that having no control makes you mad. It isn't fair. Your daughter is supposed to be happy and healthy. You give her everything and you love her to pieces. How could this have happened? Sometimes, it just does. You have got to get yourself together to face this challenge. It will get easier, but it still stinks. There are groups and resources for parents with children dealing with mental illness. Use them.

This is what Megan's mom needs. She loves her daughter, but she is frustrated that the disease hasn't gone away, anxious that all the days of lost work caused by the illness may result in her losing her job, and angry that she hasn't seen much progress with the illness in spite of all that they have done. Talking to a group of people going through the same difficulties could be really helpful for her. Talking to other parents whose children have the same illness, but might be experiencing it at different stages can be incredibly helpful. They often have great tips and can offer hope that treatment can make a positive difference.

Action 3: Deal with your anger and anxiety so they don't culminate in anger at your daughter or shutting down when your daughter needs you.

One great way to deal with anxiety is to become an expert about your daughter's illness. Similar to managing the diagnosis of a learning disability, the more you understand your daughter's illness, the better equipped you will be to handle it. Here are some questions to ask her counselor or doctor:

- What is her diagnosis?
- What exactly does it mean?
- Is this a chronic illness, or is it likely to go away?
- How did you determine that this was her diagnosis?
- Are there any symptoms we should watch out for?

- Is there anything we can do at home to make the illness more manageable?
- Is there a medication that might help? If so, what are the likely benefits and risks?
- Are there any alternative therapies that might help?
- Is there anything that seems to make the illness worse?
- Is the illness likely to affect her academic progress?

These questions should help you to get your head around what your daughter's diagnosis means and how it is likely to affect her. Ask as many questions as you can think of until you feel as though you really understand what is going on with your daughter. No question is stupid. Mental illness is serious and seems scarier when you don't understand it. The more you know, the less intimidating it becomes.

As important as it is to become an expert so you can help your daughter understand her illness and advocate for herself, it is really important not to get obsessed or surf the web all night looking for solutions. There are a few key sites at the end of the chapter that have great links to resources. Be careful of some of the websites you might come across if you just put your child's disorder into a search engine. There are some unhelpful sites—sites that will make you worry more than you need to, or sites that can give false hope. Try and limit your time searching the Internet for information. Find a few helpful and legitimate sites and stick to those sites. Your daughter's pediatrician and anyone else treating her should be able to direct you to helpful resources as well.

Action 4: Learn all about your daughter's diagnosis. Become an expert.

Now that you understand the diagnosis, it is important that your daughter understands it as well. Her healthcare providers should help her with this, and they should also be able to help you with language you can use to effectively discuss her illness with her. Subjects that you should discuss with her include the definition of her diagnosis, the symptoms of the diagnosis, how medicines she may be taking are supposed to help, coping strategies, how to be alert to worsening symptoms, privacy, and safe people she can talk to if she feels her symptoms are worsening.

Megan already knows that her diagnosis is OCD and that her symptoms include hand washing. What she didn't realize, however, was that her OCD had other symptoms, too. For example, when she becomes really anxious, she first starts to scratch her shoulder—not hard, but it is almost like a precursor to feeling the compulsion to wash her hands. She learned that once she started to do this, she needed to implement a stress-reducing or symptom-management strategy right away. This helped Megan begin to recognize the physical course of her illness, and enabled her to soon label the feeling she was having prior to the shoulder scratching so that she could start intervening even before the shoulder scratching began.

It is sometimes very difficult for children to understand how their emotions can lead to a physical manifestation of hand washing, cutting, fighting, and so on, so it is really important to help them learn to label how they are feeling. For example, Megan believed that when she felt dirty or thought her hands weren't clean enough, she was compelled to wash them and that was that. In reality, the feelings of being unclean, or needing to wash her hands were related to her stress level. By monitoring when she washed her hands, how long it took her to stop washing them, and what she was doing just prior to the hand washing, she was able to see that there was often a stressful event or stressful thoughts about school that led up to the dirty thoughts that then led to her hand washing. It was really helpful for her to learn how to recognize her stress level and when it was increasing. It was also really helpful for her parents to see what things stressed Megan out. They hadn't recognized that things they thought were fun for Megan were often the culprits.

Your daughter should know where she could go for help when she begins feeling her symptoms; this person should be someone who understands her illness. She might want to talk to her neighbor about her medicines because the neighbor always gives her candy, but the neighbor might not be the best choice. Coming up with a list of people she can talk to in a variety of settings can be helpful. Ideally, there should be a person she can talk to in every setting where she spends a substantial amount of time. The nurse or guidance counselor at school, the assistant coach at swimming, your sister-in-law at family events, and the codirector at camp are all good examples of persons she might be able to talk to safely. It is important that you let them know that you decided, with your daughter's help, that these adults are safe, trustworthy people for her to talk to when she is struggling. Make sure they are open to it and feel comfortable being that designated person. Do make sure that these people are trustworthy and won't gossip about your daughter, that they know some of her stress or symptom-management techniques, and that they are equipped to handle anything she may tell them. If you have a daughter who is struggling with suicidal ideation, it is really important that the safe adults around her know to call you and a local emergency service if they are concerned by what she is telling them.

If your daughter is taking medication, educate her on how the medicine is supposed to be helping her. She might see it as something horrible that she is forced to take every night that makes her stomach upset. If she can appreciate that this same medicine is the medicine that helps her stop obsessing or feeling so unmotivated, she might not mind any negative side effects as much. Some kids don't have negative side effects; they simply don't want to take medicine because it is a pain in the neck. Try and point out the benefits and positive changes you see when she does take her medicine. If your daughter is taking medicine, certain people may need to know—such as the school nurse. This isn't something you need to tell everyone, however, or that your daughter needs to tell everyone. Kids can be mean. Her friend who finds out about her mood stabilizer may be the same girl six months from now who is her enemy and tells everyone that your daughter is crazy because she takes medicine. It is horrible to have to think this way, but it is the unfortunate way of the world at times.

With many illnesses comes an array of coping strategies, which can be incredibly helpful. They may include taking a quick time-out, deep breathing, visualizations, distraction techniques, and talking to a safe adult. You, your daughter, and your daughter's providers should be able to come up with a nice list of options. Megan had a tiny wooden shamrock that she kept in her pocket at all times. When she would feel particularly anxious at school, she would rub the wood between her fingers. It distracted her and soothed her enough so that she could make it through class. Little things like these can often make big differences. Make sure she is familiar with her coping skills and understands when to put them into action.

A quick word on privacy; kids can be chatty. Some health information may be best left unreported to the entire fifth-grade class. Like in the example described above, someone who is a friend one day will be an enemy the next and use confidential information against your daughter. In addition, medicines are being passed around in circles of friends like candy. It could be best for your daughter if others don't know what she is taking. Keep all medicines locked in a safe place. If she has friends over who are curious about her medicine, you would be surprised at how many wouldn't think twice about trying one out. Talk to her about privacy. Her diagnosis is nothing to be ashamed of, but it is something to be kept private, as sometimes other kids don't know how to use that kind of information appropriately.

Action 5: Discuss the illness with your daughter so she understands what it is, how to recognize the symptoms, and how to implement coping strategies.

What if you started off like Megan's mom? Can you bounce back? Yes. Your daughter might be a bit wary of you for a while, but you can bounce back. One of the best things to do, no matter how you dealt with her illness in the beginning, is to check in with her from time to time. Have a safe space in your house, or in your car (potentially the best place to talk to kids since they don't have to make eye contact with you!) and just ask, "Hey, how are things going? Have you been feeling okay?" Your daughter might open up or she might not. It is still important to do this every week or so—and more frequently if she is not doing particularly well. Follow up your question about how she is doing with a reminder, "I hope you know I love you and I want to be as supportive as I can. This is a learning process for me, too, so if you have any tips, let me in on them!" Reminding her that you love her and that you want to help her can be annoying, but you are better off annoying her with love and affection than sending her mixed messages by ignoring or avoiding the issue.

Action 6: Check in with your daughter consistently by asking her how she is and reminding her that you love and support her.

Stay active in your daughter's treatment. Even when she is on an upswing, it is important to stay connected to her providers and to your own support systems. Mental illness can be quite unpredictable. It isn't anyone's fault that it flares up at times, so you need to roll with it. Can you try to keep things as stable as possible? Absolutely!! But don't be upset or focus on your frustration when you hit a bump in the road. Accept it and keep moving forward. Don't try and place blame if no one is at fault.

Action 7: Stay active in treatment and be ready for flare-ups!

Anxiety: This is a big one that seems to be popping up everywhere. You hear about panic attacks and fears as much as you hear about braces and glasses. Megan's OCD is in the family of anxiety disorders, and more and more kids seem to be affected by anxiety these days. This shouldn't come as too much of a surprise since many of the adults around them are pretty anxious. We live in a stressed out society, and stress is trickling—or pouring—down on our kids.

> "Anxiety disorders are among the most common mental, emotional, and behavioral problems to occur during childhood and adolescence. About 13 of every 100 children and adolescents ages nine to seventeen experience some kind of anxiety disorder; girls are affected more than boys. About half of children and adolescents with anxiety disorders have a second anxiety disorder or other mental or behavioral disorder, such as depression." Substance Abuse and Mental Health Services Association.

Anxiety is one of the disorders that make people around the anxious person absolutely crazy. Anxious people can be annoying. They tend to cancel plans, and they can be fine one minute and a disaster the next. It is not easy to be friends with an anxious person, and it is really not easy to be the parent of an anxious child. In childhood, anxiety often manifests itself physically and *only* physically because children rarely have the ability to express that they are anxious. You might know that they are anxious, but they are not sophisticated enough to know that the physical sensations they have are due to anxiety. You may hear statements such as: "My stomach hurts," "my head hurts," "I can't see straight," "I can't sleep," "I'm not hungry," and "I can't breathe." Sweating, diarrhea, vomiting, weight loss, and even seizures may accompany these statements. Together, these statements and physical reactions look like a pretty scary medical issue, and can be, so it is imperative even if you think your child's symptoms are caused by anxiety, that you bring her to a doctor and make sure there is nothing physically wrong with her.

Batteries of tests may reveal nothing, which one would think would bring a sigh of relief. Not always. If there is nothing *wrong*, then what *is* wrong? How do you fix the headaches? What do you do about the seizures? There is no magic pill; there is no perfect course of treatment. There are medications, stress reduction techniques, therapy, and there is hope, but none are a quick fix. This is why anxiety can make you mad. If it is "just anxiety," shouldn't she be able to get over it? Can't you push her hard enough to work through it? One would hope so, but that is not the usual outcome. Think about it; you know how anxiety feels and you can label the feelings you have as anxiety. You are also older and not as self-conscious as you were growing up; you have learned how to cope with anxiety. Imagine how it must feel to be a little girl who knows that whenever she has a test, her head will hurt and she won't be able to breathe. Her anxiety may appear at random times; she may have seizures for no reason. That alone will cause her more anxiety. It takes time to teach a child how to recognize anxiety, know when it might occur, master coping techniques, and then use them appropriately.

Another problem with anxiety is that it is really hard to figure out when to push a kid and when to go easy on her. It changes by the day and by the event. Megan missing a school dance provides a perfect example. Maybe she missed the dance and was absolutely fine with it. But maybe she missed the dance and wished she had gone. What would have happened if her parents had forced her to go? She may have spent the night feeling anxious, wishing she could wash her hands, and calling you for a ride home. Alternatively, she could have gone and been distracted by all the fun she was having. It is a really tough call, and every child is different. Of course, you don't want your child to miss out on events, but you also don't want to send her into a situation where she is going to freak out so much that it will be a long time before she is willing to try anything new again. One way to manage this is to push her to go to certain events—with an out. If she is anxious about a party, tell her you will wait outside for thirty minutes to make sure she is comfortable. If she has school anxiety, work with the school on getting her re-engaged one class at a time. Definitely work with her providers to help find a balance that will eventually get her as active a life as possible.

Anxiety often begs the question—is she faking it? It can seem like a convenient disorder at times. What if your daughter is anxious at school to the point that she has full-blown panic attacks that land her in the nurse's office, but she can party with the best of them every weekend without so much as a shudder? Should you let her go to the parties? Is she manipulating you? What if her anxiety keeps the family from doing things her siblings love, but whenever you do things that she loves, she is fine? These sorts of things are also difficult. Again, you don't want to cause her more anxiety, but at the same time it isn't fair that her siblings miss out. This is really tricky. There are absolutely times when she may be manipulating you or exaggerating her symptoms. As you get to know her disorder better, and work with her providers, you will figure out when to push, when to ease up, when to set consequences, and when to be more forgiving.

Anxiety is a serious illness that can get worse if the appropriate treatments are not put into place. It is scary and overwhelming for the child and the parent. Don't let yourself or your daughter be held hostage by her illness. Find ways to work with her illness and improve her quality of life. Don't let her use it as a crutch to get out of things she doesn't want to do. It is a fine line, and you might goof from time to time, but you will figure it out eventually. Be patient.

Chapter 10:
Action Recap

Action 1: If you are concerned that your daughter may have a mental illness, take her to see her primary care physician or another health professional.

Action 2: Understand that you cannot control your child's mental illness. But you can do your best to provide a supportive environment for your child.

Action 3: Deal with your anger and anxiety so they don't culminate in anger at your daughter or shutting down when your daughter needs you.

Action 4: Learn all about your daughter's diagnosis. Become an expert.

Action 5: Discuss the illness with your daughter so she understands what it is, how to recognize the symptoms, and how to implement coping strategies.

Action 6: Check in with your daughter consistently by asking her how she is and reminding her that you love and support her.

Action 7: Stay active in treatment and be ready for flare-ups!

Chapter 10:
Top Five Talking Points

1. I know I am a worrywart, but sometimes you just don't seem like yourself. I think it is important that we go to see your primary care physician, just to be sure everything is going okay.

2. I know you are dealing with a lot, but sometimes I get really frustrated because I don't know how to help you. This isn't your fault. You might have to be patient with me while I try to figure out how to be the best support I can be for you. If you have any ideas, let me know!

3. I thought we should talk a little bit about your diagnosis. Do you have any questions or concerns about it? Is there anything you are worried about or that upsets you about it?

4. I know you love your friends, and I think they are great, too. I would still just be careful about how much you tell them when it comes to your diagnosis, medication, and counseling. They might accidentally say something to someone else that you don't want others knowing.

5. We do need to make sure that there is someone at school and in the after-school program who knows about your medicine and a little bit about what is going on. Do you have anyone in mind?

Chapter 10: *Resources*

http://mentalhealth.samhsa.gov/

This is the Substance Abuse and Mental Health Services Administration
website. You can find just about anything on any type of disorder. It is a
great resource.

http://www.nami.org/

This is the National Alliance on Mental Illness website. Here you can find
easy-to-understand explanations of different mental illnesses, support
groups for parents of children with mental illness, and much more. The
site also has resources for those diagnosed with a mental illness.

http://www.nimh.nih.gov/index.shtml

This is the rather research-heavy website from the National Institute of
Mental Health. If you like facts and reading, this could be the one for
you.

ELEVEN

Death and Loss

Because there are many resources for dealing with the loss of a parent or sibling that provide comprehensive information that can help your daughter work through such a loss, this chapter will instead focus on other sorts of losses. However, all losses can cause pain, and sometimes the death of someone outside the family may be felt as deeply or even more deeply by some children than if they had occurred within the family.

"Gracie has been crying for a week. She didn't even know this kid. I think she went to one party with him. I don't understand why his death is such a big deal to her. It isn't like her best friend died. This is a bit over the top if you ask me." Gracie's mother shook her head in frustration.

Gracie crossed her arms over her chest and glared. "I went to two parties with him. He was at Jimmy's bowling party in second grade and Alicia's party last year. He has been in school with me for *eight years*. Even the teachers told us we might be surprised by how upset we might feel, even if we didn't know him very well."

"Well, maybe you wouldn't feel so bad if your teachers hadn't said that. I have never heard you even talk about him. Why is this affecting you so much?"

Gracie's teachers and Gracie are on to something. When kids lose someone they only know as an acquaintance, it can still be very significant for them. For Gracie, this loss was her first of someone her age and the first of someone from her school. In addition, it happened as a result of a very sudden, tragic accident. All of these factors made the loss huge for Gracie. She was actually handling it better than her mom. Someone crying for a week after such a loss isn't that unusual. Gracie was twelve years old when her classmate died. The thought that someone in her class would all of a sudden be taken had never crossed her mind. Gracie needed help and support in dealing with her schoolmate's death. So did Mom. Not many adults handle death well. Mom seemed to want the problem to just go away. As a parent, having a child in her daughter's class die so suddenly frightened her because it reminded her that kids aren't always safe. We do our best to protect them, but we can't keep them in a bubble. She ended up becoming quite anxious about Gracie's safety and eventually recognizing that the loss of this peer of Gracie's impacted her quite a bit, even though she really didn't know the young man.

Everyone experiences loss at some point. We prepare for the loss of grandparents, ailing elderly, and anyone who is very seriously ill. We don't prepare for sudden losses of adults or children. Those losses take us by surprise. We are somewhat prepared for loss after an illness, but we rarely talk about loss due to suicide or other tragedies. We are never fully prepared for losses of these types. But once the person is gone, there is something missing. For Gracie, it could have been not seeing him at his usual lunch table, an empty seat in homeroom, or looking at her second-grade class picture and realizing the little boy in the picture would never have his picture taken again. It is tough to deal with death, regardless of the circumstances. As a parent, you need to know how to respond to your daughter's needs while also being conscious of your own needs.

Action 1: Recognize that your daughter will eventually have to deal with death and that you will be the one to help her through that time.

How might you discuss death with your daughter? Age and maturity have a lot to do with how you should speak to her about death. It is important to be direct about death. Suggesting that the person went on a trip to heaven, or that the angels took him away, or making any sort of suggestion like that can be very confusing to your daughter. She may think that if the person who died went on a trip to heaven, he may be coming back. If you tell her that the angels took him, she could become fearful that angels will take her, too. Also, as your daughter gets older, she is going to know that you are lying and just trying to make death sound better. Be direct. State that the person died and ask if she has any questions. For example, if her grandmother dies, say, "Jenny, I have to share some sad news with you. Grammie died today. I know this is the first time you have had someone you love die, and I want you to know that I am here for you if you need a hug or if you have any questions."

Action 2: Be direct. Don't give confusing explanations.

Let her know that you are there for her, no matter how well she knew the person or how sad she seems. Just knowing that you are there for her is likely to be extremely helpful to her. Address the fact that she has experienced a death. If the person who died is not someone you know, don't avoid the subject and just assume she is fine since she didn't bring it up. You should bring it up. Inform her that you heard someone she knew had died. She might want to know how you heard this information, what people are saying about the death, and more. Make sure she knows that she can ask you any questions she may have about it.

Action 3: Acknowledge the death and let her know that you are sorry about her loss.

What if she asks a ton of questions? She probably will. Her questions might not come right away; they might come weeks later. Be prepared and willing to answer questions even if they come much later. How much detail should you provide? This is a personal decision. It may turn on your religion, spirituality, and how the person died. However, it is still important to be direct and not say anything that would frighten her. Try to avoid unnecessary details about the death, such as, "She was dead for three days before anyone found her in her bathtub." Statements like these are likely to horrify a child. You might think, "Of course I wouldn't say that to her!" But keep in mind that little ears like to eavesdrop around times of family stress; saying something like that on the phone to one of your friends or relatives could easily be overheard.

If the person died after a long illness, the death might be a little easier to explain. "Gram's illness was really painful for her; eventually, her body got too tired to fight it." Your child might then ask, "You say you are tired all the time. Is that going to happen to you, too?" An easy answer is, "I am tired a lot, but that is very different. Gram's body was sick. I just need more sleep!!"

If someone dies suddenly, it is a little easier to explain if they are older, "Sometimes as our bodies get older, they don't work as well as they used to and they stop working." Your child might then ask, "Are you going to die? You always say you are getting older." Or, "Am I going to die? I will be ten next week!!" Your answer could be, "Dying isn't something you should worry about. I am getting older, but my body is still working well!"

If someone dies in a tragic accident, there is no need to tell all the details to your daughter. However, if it was a public tragedy (a big car accident, a murder, etc.), it is likely that your daughter is going to see a news story or hear bits and pieces of information or rumors that are pretty descriptive and often scary. It is important that you be there for her if those questions arise. "Cassie died today in an accident. You might hear people talking about the accident because a lot of people know and love Cassie. I want you to come to me with any questions or anything you hear that scares you or worries you, okay?" If she is hearing awful things from particular people, it is perfectly acceptable for you to pull those adults aside and ask them to refrain from giving your daughter unnecessary details as these sorts of details might be very traumatic for her to hear. If she asks questions about things she is hearing, you can reinforce that it is important to focus on the nice things she remembers about the person who has passed away, "I know some of the things people are saying about Cassie's accident are pretty awful. You should try to focus instead on nice ways to remember Cassie—like how nice she was to people, or her beautiful smile, okay?"

If the death was a suicide, you can follow the advice from the example above, but also use it as a way to open up a discussion about mental illness. DO NOT let your daughter think that suicide *happens* to people. Talk to her about depression: "It is terrible that John felt so awful that he felt like suicide was the only option for him. I want you to know that if you ever feel that way, you can talk to me about it and I will not be angry or upset. I will help you in any way that I can. It is important that you know that you always have someone to talk to; if you don't want to talk to me, we can find someone else for you to talk to. I won't mind at all." Suicide is an incredibly difficult topic because so many times the person who died is glorified in death. Kids notice this and think, "Look at him. Everyone loves him now that he is gone. He is a hero." They forget that the person who died will never know that people are now viewing him as a hero, or that this person left behind people who care for him and will be forever impacted by his death. Be aware of what kind of publicity this kind of death gets at school and in the community.

Action 4: Be available to answer your daughter's questions with straightforward answers. Try and control any rumors or excessive talk about how the person died. It is okay for her to know some details, but most are unnecessary.

Hopefully, your daughter won't have to deal with the death of a classmate. But it can happen. When a peer dies, it is often very confusing for a child because it makes the child realize that she could die. Kids usually think that only the elderly or those who are sick die. When a classmate, friend, or peer dies, it can be really overwhelming to them. Your child might develop fears after a death. For younger children, having a classmate die in a car accident can make them afraid to ride in a car because cars are now associated with death. If a younger child has a friend who dies of an illness, you may find that she becomes hypervigilant for a while about any tiny little cough or pain. This kind of behavior is really normal. If it doesn't go away, however, you might take your daughter to speak to a counselor.

Action 5: Be prepared for fears about death to crop up, especially if the person who died is the same age as your daughter.

Many parents are concerned about how their own reactions to death might affect their daughter. "What if I am really upset by a death? What should I do? I don't want to cry in front of her." Why not? If you cry in front of your daughter, your daughter will see that you are human. There is nothing wrong with crying, or mourning, or taking a day off from work. Your reaction may help your daughter see that it is okay to be sad about losing someone. She will also see that life still goes on and people recover. If you hide your emotions, she is going to think that there is something wrong with having emotions. Even if you think you can hide your emotions better than anyone else, she probably knows you better than you think and will be able to sense that something is up. If you are having a difficult time with the loss, talking to someone like a counselor can benefit you as well as those who love you.

Action 6: Allow yourself to grieve. Don't hide your emotions from your daughter.

Wakes, funerals, vigils, and memorials; these are all a part of what comes along with someone dying. You should reflect thoughtfully on whether your daughter's attendance at such events is a good idea. Take into account her age, her relationship with the person, her ability to handle a sad event, the type of ceremony, your emotional well-being, and the emotional well-being of others she knows who will be at the ceremony. For example, if you and your siblings are having a difficult time and you know you won't be able to respond to your eight-year-old daughter's needs at the funeral, she shouldn't go. This is not because she won't be able to handle it. It is because seeing all the people she loves incredibly distraught isn't fair to her or to you and your other family members. You may need to take care of your own grieving, and to lose it if that would be helpful to you. This doesn't mean you will hide your grief from your daughter; it is just a way to allow yourself space for your own processing of grief without having to worry about how she is doing. If you can pull it together, or if there is a cousin who can keep her eye on your daughter during the ceremony, maybe bringing her will be fine.

When you consider bringing her to something like this, definitely keep in mind who will be there and if her presence will make it harder for others to grieve in the way they need to or if it could potentially help them get through it. It is also important that you consider her ability to handle the situation. Is she a crier? Is she overly sensitive? Does she obsess or ruminate over sad things? Maybe attending the services is not the best way for her to pay her respects. The type of service is also important. If it is a closed casket or open casket, a full mass funeral or a memorial service, a candlelight vigil, or something very private—these are important facts to know and should definitely factor into your decision.

Before making your mind up and stressing out on how to tell her she can or cannot go, ask her what she would like to do. Don't ask her in front of anyone or in a way that suggests how you want her to answer ("You don't want to go, do you?"). Just ask her how she feels about going. Is she afraid to go? Is there anything about going that worries her? She may not want to go and you could be her out. She may also have fears that the wake is open casket, or that she would feel odd at the funeral of someone whose religion differs from hers. Allow her time and space to ask any questions she may have about the services. Hear her out when she explains why she does or does not want to go. Be as supportive as you can about her decision even if you would have preferred that she decided differently.

When a peer has died, find out if the school or other parents are getting together to attend the services or to hold their own memorial. Sometimes it is nice for kids who have experienced a loss to experience the services together; however, there still needs to be adult supervision at the services. You can attend the services, or wait outside the funeral home with other parents, but it is important that someone accompany your daughter to something that can be so emotionally charged. Kids can be great supports, but often if one crumbles, the rest crumble as well. An adult or many adults should be available in case this happens.

There are many ways a child can honor or respect someone who has died without attending a ceremony. If a classmate's parent dies, a card and an invitation out for ice cream might be a perfect solution. You could call the other parent and see if a play date would help the other child during this time. Perhaps planting a tree, delivering cookies, or making a home-cooked meal, would make your daughter feel as though she is sending her best wishes. She doesn't have to go to the services to show that she cares for the family of the person who died.

Action 7: Decide, with the help of your daughter, whether it is a good idea for her to attend the services.

Enough is enough!! What happens if your daughter is mourning and mourning and mourning? She could be a slow mourner. This is okay unless it keeps her from school, going to activities, or otherwise prevents her from functioning. She could also get sad seemingly out of the blue. Remember, grief doesn't happen and then go away; it is a process and everyone's grieving is very different. Your daughter might seem totally fine for the first week or even the first month. Then, all of a sudden, she may be sad. Some girls don't become sad; instead, they become irritable and angry. They also don't always know that they are sad, mad, angry, or irritable because of a death or loss. Your daughter might recognize that she is irritable but not even relate it to the death of a student in her school. It could really catch her off guard. Be prepared to help her identify the source of her feelings if she needs insight.

It's unlikely that you will be able to predict how a death or different deaths might affect her. She might seem fine when a close relative dies, but be devastated when a distant cousin dies. Whatever her process, try and give her the space to let it unfold at her pace. Let her know that you are there for her if she wants to talk, needs a distraction, or just wants to sit with you. Ask her if there is anything you can do to help her through this time, or to make her feel better. If it seems like she is experiencing mourning too slowly, or that it is lingering on, find her a counselor to talk to who can help her work through it in a productive way.

Action 8: Let her grief run its course, but if it is keeping her from her regular activities, find someone who can help her.

Chapter 11:
Action Recap

Action 1: Recognize that your daughter will eventually have to deal with death and that you will be the one to help her through that time.

Action 2: Be direct. Don't give confusing explanations.

Action 3: Acknowledge the death and let her know that you are sorry for her loss.

Action 4: Be available to answer your daughter's questions with straightforward answers. Try to control any rumors or excessive talk about how the person died. It is okay for her to know some details, but most are unnecessary.

Action 5: Be prepared for fears about death to crop up, especially if the person who died is the same age as your daughter.

Action 6: Allow yourself to grieve. Don't hide your emotions from your daughter.

Action 7: Decide, with the help of your daughter, whether it is a good idea for her to attend the services.

Action 8: Let her grief run its course, but if it is keeping her from her regular activities, find someone who can help her.

Chapter 11:
Top Five Talking Points

1. I heard Veronica in your class died in an accident. I am so sorry. Do you want to talk about it?

2. I hope you know I am here for you if you want to ask any questions or if you want me to just sit with you if you aren't feeling very well.

3. Sometimes rumors start and people talk about details of death that really are not important. Remember your friend as she was, not in the way that people are talking about her now.

4. I heard from Jenna's mom that there is going to be a wake tomorrow night. Do you want to go? [Let her answer] I understand why you might want to go. I would be glad to drive you and your friends to the wake if you would like, and to wait outside while you and your friends attend. I want to be sure that you and your friends are okay. Dealing with the death of someone you know can be really tough.

5. Grief is a really tough process. You have been particularly cranky lately, and I think the way you are feeling has to do with losing Auntie. I know it has been a couple of months, but you still seem pretty upset about it. Why don't we find a counselor who can meet with you to discuss how you are feeling about her death?

TWELVE

The Curious Case of Drugs and Alcohol

Cori and her mother sat in the room, refusing to speak to one another. Cori, a vivacious, sometimes snarky, very bright, well-liked eleven-year-old, sat on her hands and swung her legs uneasily. Mom stared out the window while she thought out loud, "I just don't understand it. She is eleven. What on earth could an eleven-year-old want with drugs? It doesn't make sense to me."

Cori had tried huffing with her friends. They had seen a video on the Internet about how to huff; they thought it looked pretty harmless and kind of funny. It involved inhaling canned air. How dangerous could canned air be? It was dangerous enough that Cori passed out, vomited, and choked on her own vomit. Luckily, her friends called 9-1-1 and alerted a neighbor who helped them out. Cori was kept overnight in the hospital for observation, and her parents were encouraged to seek counseling for her.

This was an unusual case in that Cori hadn't been experimenting with drugs prior to that day. She had been curious about drugs, and had tried smoking a cigarette, but she hadn't tried alcohol or any other drugs. Usually, when kids get caught, it isn't their first time experimenting. It was also unusual for a child to be brought in for counseling right after such an experience. Usually, adults expect a certain amount of experimentation. Often, the first few signs that a child has tried something are ignored, or are addressed with a stern lecture. Such instances don't usually result in an immediate trip to a therapist. In this case, Mom was concerned about Cori's use, but what seemed to alarm her most was Cori's age. She never saw it coming and brought Cori to counseling for Cori's benefit and hers as well. Mom had given her a minilecture that went something like this, "Drugs and drinking are bad. Don't do them. You will end up dropping out of high school." And that was that. That wasn't a bad start, but Mom needed to continue the conversation and make it a little less one-sided. Perhaps she should have opened up the topic for discussion instead of just making a statement and avoiding a discussion.

When should you start the conversation? You should start it when your daughter is quite young! If eleven seems young to you as far as conversations about drugs and alcohol go, think again. According to the National Inhalant Prevention Coalition's website, nearly one of every five kids has abused an inhalant by seventh grade. That is really scary. Seventh-graders are usually twelve or thirteen. The average drinking age is also getting progressively younger. The National Institute on Alcohol Abuse and Alcoholism published an article in January 2006 that reported, "In 2003 the average age of first use of alcohol was about 14, compared to about 17 in 1965." Also included in this article were statistics gathered in 2005 by Monitoring the Future that stated, "three-fourths of 12th graders, more than two-thirds of 10th graders, and about two in every five

8th graders have consumed alcohol." Following this statement was a very scary statistic:

> **"11 percent of 8th graders, 22 percent of 10th graders, and 29 percent of 12th graders had engaged in heavy episodic (or "binge") drinking within the past two weeks."**

Can you imagine your eighth-grader binge drinking? How old is an eighth-grader? Thirteen? Fourteen? That would mean approximately four drinks in an hour for a male or five over two hours for a female. This is scary stuff and very real. If your daughter isn't drinking or thinking about it, her friends are or someone she knows is drinking or thinking about it. Drugs and alcohol are everywhere; they aren't a one-conversation type of topic. Drugs and alcohol require ongoing conversations and reminders. To keep an ongoing dialogue going, you will need to mentally prepare yourself to have the conversation and keep informed about trends in drug and alcohol use.

Check out the resources at the end of the chapter, and ask school personnel and emergency responders about drug trends in your area. Cities and towns seem to have variable drug cultures. One town might be known as a big cocaine town, while the city next door has a widespread huffing issue among its younger citizens. You don't have to become obsessed with drug trends, but it is important to have an idea of the drugs that are more abundant in your city or town.

Action 1: Mentally prepare and brush up on drug and alcohol trends to ready yourself to have a conversation about drugs and alcohol with your daughter.

How will you know what to discuss with your daughter? Should you just make a statement like Cori's mom? No. Ask your daughter what she knows about drugs and alcohol. What has she been told by friends, at school, or by others about drugs and alcohol? Are her friends using anything or talking about trying things out? Does she know anyone who has? Ask out of curiosity, not to accuse her of anything. It will help you to know what she knows about drugs and alcohol and how she perceives drugs and alcohol. She could know more than you, she could be misinformed, or drugs and alcohol could be the last things on her mind. You won't know unless you ask, and have an open conversation with her about it.

Before you ask her, set up a nonpunishment zone. Make sure she knows the conversation is punishment and judgment free; she will not get grounded if she tells you incriminating information in this conversation. And mean it!! Allow her to ask questions and tell you her fears about drugs and alcohol without the fear that she is going to get grounded for coming clean. If she tells you that she has experimented, let her know that the next time she experiments, she will be grounded or there will be other consequences. But this conversation is punishment free. This will help establish your expectations and help her understand what will happen if she does experiment or continues to experiment.

Action 2: Have a conversation with your daughter that is educational, nonjudgmental, punishment free, allows her to ask questions, and sets out future expectations and rules.

Cori was misinformed. Cori and her friends thought they were inhaling air, just in a purer form. They didn't realize there were chemicals in the canned air that can be deadly. Those chemicals can be deadly the first time you huff or the twentieth time. There is no telling how huffing will affect a person's body. It sounds so innocent, but it is incredibly dangerous, and extremely accessible. Cori and her friends made assumptions that many kids make; if you can buy it at a store without identification, it can't be that bad!!

Kids think similarly about over-the-counter medications. If a store sells it, it must be safe. Keep this in mind when you talk about drugs and alcohol with your daughter. Parents often forget about the drugs that are easy to access, such as prescription medication that is in your house, over-the-counter medications, inhalants, and tobacco products. Don't forget the seemingly innocent drugs when you talk to your daughter.

Action 3: Don't forget to include prescription, over-the-counter medicines, and tobacco products in your conversations.

As mentioned earlier, this is not a one-conversation type of subject. Talk about it often. Bring up current events that involve people entering rehab or a local drunk-driving accident. Ask her what the kids in her grade are doing? Are they starting to experiment? Has anyone been in any trouble? Hug her before she leaves the house and say, "No drugs, no drinking, no cigarettes, and I love you." You might sound like a broken record, but remember that the squeaky wheel gets the goods!!!

If you keep the conversation going, not only are you reminding her that you are aware that kids experiment, but you also let her know that you care and don't want her to use. If you are bringing it up, it could encourage her to open up if she has a concern about something. It is much easier to bring up a concern in the midst of a conversation instead of having to initiate the conversation herself. Also, as kids get older, the conversation changes. Maybe her friends weren't using in sixth grade, but over the summer the experimentation started. Now there is more pressure for her to use and she will need more guidance and support from you. Find out who her friends are, what they are doing, and who is supervising them. Are you going to sound annoying? Yup. Is that your job as a parent? Yup. If you are concerned about her choices in friends because you know three of them were just suspended for bringing Kahlúa to lunch to put in their chocolate milk, you are right to be concerned! Does this mean these kids are hoodlums and horrible children? No. But they might not be the kids you want her hanging at the park with unsupervised on a Friday evening. So as you keep the conversation going with her, make sure you find out about her friends and their lifestyles.

The Substance Abuse and Mental Health Services Administration (SAMHSA) has one of the best websites for parents to get pointers on talking to their kids about alcohol. They have a program called *Talk Early, Talk Often, Get Others Involved,* which has tons of great tips, reasons why you should talk to your child early and often, who to involve (school, community, and others), and pointers on how to get the conversation going. There is even a way to develop an action plan on how to have the conversation with your child. Most often resources will be at the end of a chapter, but this resource goes above and beyond, and is filled with great information for parents. If you don't have a computer or access to the Internet, it is worth going to a local community center or library just to use a computer where you can check out this website: http://www.underagedrink ing.samhsa.gov/.

Hooray for great resources like SAMHSA and others who can really help parents and other adults connect with their children about touchy subjects like drugs and alcohol.

Action 4: Keep the conversations about alcohol and drugs going.

Talking about drugs and alcohol is one way to prevent use. Another way is to role model appropriate behavior. Your behaviors and conversations make a difference in your child's life. According to SAMHSA's website, "over 70% of children say parents are the leading influence in their decision to drink or not."

That is a pretty significant percentage. So even if you think your daughter lets things go in one ear and out the other, and that she pays little or no attention to you, she does hear you sometimes. She might not remember your favorite ice cream flavor. She might not remember you told her about the family party for Great Aunt Bea. But she probably remembers what you say and what you do when it comes to drugs and alcohol.

And oh boy, if they don't line up with each other, get ready for a bit of a battle. If you tell her about the horrors of drinking and how binge drinking is bad, and then you go out with your girlfriends, get a buzz on, drive home, and get all giggly—just wait until she comes home buzzed or drunk for the first time. You'd better believe that any lecture you try on her is going to be met with, "Oh really? What about the time that *you* came home buzzed? Didn't you *drive*? I didn't drive. I was smart enough to take a cab." You won't have a leg to stand on. Start to think about your actions. She is observing you and the other adults in her life. Maybe you don't drink, but maybe her favorite aunt smokes marijuana here and there and it is a bit of a family joke. Is it even funny? Not really. If it is dealt with so lightly in the family, do you think your daughter will see it as a big deal if she starts smoking here and there? Probably not.

Lead by example and encourage others to do the same. Is her aunt going to quit marijuana and become the perfect role model? Not necessarily, but you can certainly let her aunt know that you don't want her smoking or being high around your daughter, and that you are going to let your daughter know that you don't approve of those actions. If her aunt can't respect that, then you will need to decide if her aunt is a safe person for her to be around without supervision.

Action 5: Be a good role model, and surround her with other positive role models.

What can you help your daughter do to avoid peer pressure and the temptation of experimentation? Talk to her about how to say "no." Role model a drug and alcohol abuse–free way of life. Teach her how to have fun. It sounds odd, but some kids don't know how to keep themselves busy. Idle time is not always great. Should your daughter have down time to just chill? Of course!! But she also needs to learn how to entertain herself.

For some kids, the option to smoke weed in the basement is simply chosen because it is the only option, or the most exciting option. Give her options. Sign her up for after school activities. Get her involved in hobbies that she can have access to at home, such as baking, carpentry, sewing, reading, exercise, painting, or woodworking. Seriously. For some, playing ball at the park isn't an option because the park isn't safe. Staying home or at a relative's house is safer, but can often lead to boredom. When you are bored, you get into things that aren't always beneficial. Teach her how to stay entertained and make sure she has the tools to do so. If she loves to do crossword puzzles, download some from the Internet or cut them out of the newspaper. If she likes to build things, make sure she has Legos, or model planes, or popsicle sticks and glue. These hobbies could potentially cost a bit of cash, or make a bit of a mess, but a little cash here, a little glue there—much better than a little buzz here, a little high there. . . .

Action 6: Teach her how to entertain herself and make sure she has options other than drugs and alcohol.

You have educated yourself, kept the conversation happening, role modeled, and signed her up for the most fun activities in the world. She will never try drugs now, right? Unfortunately, there is no magic conversation, activity, or role model who can prevent experimentation. The best kid in the world can end up having her stomach pumped on prom night. The smartest girl in the class can get caught smoking a blunt with last year's valedictorian. No child is ever drug and alcohol proof. So what should you look for in terms of warning signs?

First of all, if your child ever has any major changes in behavior, appetite, energy, motivation, or appearance, it is important to talk to her and take her to her primary care physician if you are concerned. Second of all, don't drive yourself crazy looking for warning signs. Sometimes the warning signs of drug or alcohol use can be caused by tears shed over a boyfriend, compounded by a virus, and not enough sleep. So please, before searching for something that might not be, try and stay reasonable. Be aware of the warning signs, address any you do see, but don't look for something that isn't there.

The following signs and symptoms of alcohol or drug use and abuse are taken from the American Council for Drug Education website.

PHYSICAL SIGNS

- Loss of appetite, increase in appetite, any changes in eating habits, unexplained weight loss or gain.
- Slowed or staggering walk; poor physical coordination.
- Inability to sleep, awake at unusual times, unusual laziness.
- Red, watery eyes; pupils larger or smaller than usual; blank stare.
- Cold, sweaty palms; shaking hands.
- Puffy face, blushing, or paleness.
- Smell of substance on breath, body, or clothes.
- Extreme hyperactivity; excessive talkativeness.

- Runny nose; hacking cough.

- Needle marks on lower arm, leg, or bottom of feet.

- Nausea, vomiting, or excessive sweating.

- Tremors or shakes of hands, feet, or head.

- Irregular heartbeat.

BEHAVIORAL SIGNS

- Change in overall attitude/personality with no other identifiable cause.

- Changes in friends; new hangouts; sudden avoidance of old crowd; doesn't want to talk about new friends; friends are known drug users.

- Change in activities or hobbies.

- Drop in grades at school or performance at work; skips school or is late for school.

- Change in habits at home; loss of interest in family and family activities.

- Difficulty in paying attention; forgetfulness.

- General lack of motivation, energy, self-esteem, "I don't care" attitude.

- Sudden oversensitivity, temper tantrums, or resentful behavior.

- Moodiness, irritability, or nervousness.

- Silliness or giddiness.

- Paranoia.

- Excessive need for privacy; unreachable.

- Secretive or suspicious behavior.

- Chronic dishonesty.

- Unexplained need for money; stealing money or items.

- Change in personal grooming habits.

- Possession of drug paraphernalia.

Action 7: Get to know the warning signs of drug and alcohol use, but don't drive yourself nuts looking for what isn't there. When in doubt, take a trip to her primary care physician.

What happens if you catch her? She sleeps over at her friend's house one night and you get a phone call from her friend's mother telling you she thinks something is up because both her daughter and yours came home very giggly last night and then went right into her daughter's room to go to sleep. She thought she heard one of them throwing up in the bathroom, but she couldn't be sure. This morning, they don't look so hot. Her friend's mom tells you she is just going to let it go. Kids experiment; it is probably harmless. What will you do?

Take a deep breath. Don't freak out. Don't rush over and pull her out of her friend's house. Don't scream at the friend's mom. Collect yourself. You don't even know for sure what might have happened. It could be nothing; it could be something. The best news is that your daughter is okay. She is up, functioning, and ready to go home. Tell the other mom that you are going to come pick her up.

On the way over, think about your approach. You want to know what is going on, but you don't want to alienate your daughter or accuse her of something she may not have done. In the back of your mind, however, you suspect that she did go out drinking and now you are worried and angry. Try to keep your anxiety and anger in check. If you freak out, she isn't going to tell you anything and she will think that she can't talk to you. Decide where you will chat with her—inside a car is the best place because your daughter doesn't have to make eye contact and she is kind of stuck with you. If this is the first time you are suspicious, you could make the car a safe haven. There would be no punishment, just a conversation to find out what went on, let her know how it will be handled if it happens again, and inquire about why she felt like she needed to drink or use. If this is not the first time, and she did use alcohol or drugs, make sure you follow through on any consequences you had discussed, let her know you love her but that you are truly worried about her use, and decide on next steps such as counseling, a doctor's appointment, or drug treatment.

If you catch your daughter and she is intoxicated or high, save your breath until she is sober. Yelling at her or lecturing her when she is intoxicated or high is a waste of words. Make sure she is physically safe, and talk to her when she sobers up. Not only will you waste your breath, but also you could become angrier because she could act out, become overly emotional, or be completely obnoxious. There is also a good chance she won't remember a thing and you will just be frustrated.

Here is an example of how a conversation could go once your daughter is sober:

"Tessa, we need to talk."

Tessa looks annoyed, rubs her eyes, and glares at you. "Why?"

"I know you were drunk last night. I could smell it on your breath. You were walking crooked, and you were throwing up this morning."

"I was sick!" Tessa yells.

"Well, we are going to go to see your PCP anyway, so we can talk to her about that when we see her. You may have been sick, but I also believe you were drinking. The last time you came home drunk we talked about what would happen if you drank again. Do you remember that?"

"Yes, but I don't see what the big deal is! I don't need counseling. Ground me, that is fine, but I am not going to counseling."

"The deal was that you would go to counseling and be grounded for two weekends, and that stands. In all honesty, I think counseling is more important than the grounding."

"Well I think the counseling is stupid."

"That is fine, but you have to go. I am really worried that you are drinking so much, and I feel like you need someone to talk to, and I don't think you are comfortable talking to me about things."

"Everyone drinks this much!"

"Well, it is too much for me. Why are you drinking so much? Just because your friends are?"

"No! I had a really hard week! You have a glass of wine every Friday. Even Dad says he, 'needs a couple beers with the guys to blow off steam.'"

She has a valid point. What should your response be??

"You're right. Maybe your father and I need to learn other ways to blow off steam as well. The difference is, we are both legally allowed to drink, we don't binge drink, and we do deal with stress in other ways. You just said that you had a really hard week, and that is why you are drinking so much. That makes me think that something is really stressing you out and we have to figure out what to do to make it less stressful so you aren't looking forward to drinking and then drinking too much."

Your daughter looks at you and doesn't say anything.

"Okay. But what do I tell my friends when they ask why I am not drinking? What if they think I am a loser? What am I supposed to say? All my friends are drinking and I won't know what to do with myself when I am at a party with them. It isn't fun if I don't drink because they all act like idiots and I don't feel right being sober."

Action 8: Have a conversation or several conversations with her about her use if you find out she is using. Make sure she is sober, don't yell, ask why she is using, and follow through on consequences.

Now you are getting somewhere. By having this conversation, you now realize that your daughter is stressed out, she knows it is wrong to drink, but has noticed that both you and your husband refer to your drinking habits as ways to blow off steam. She is pressured by her friends to drink—maybe not directly, but being the only sober one can be tough for anyone, and she doesn't know how to have fun with her friends if she isn't drinking. These are some of the top reasons kids give for drinking. Now that you know her reasons, you can help her work on them.

Stress. Stress is overwhelming for everyone, but tweens tend to have a particularly difficult time with stress. At their age, they might not even understand that the feelings they have when under stress are stress. They know it doesn't feel good, but instead of labeling it stress, it could be that they feel that they can't breathe, feel like their muscles are tight, can't slow their minds down, or feel jittery. Help your daughter figure out when she is feeling stressed and either help her find some stress-relieving interventions or take her to see a counselor to help her deal with her stress.

Observation. Your daughter has observed that you and your husband think of your drinking as a way to relax. Consider pointing out other ways that you and your partner relieve stress. Instead of pouring a glass of wine and commenting, "Wooo, I had a long week. I can't wait to have my wine and unwind," pour your wine and comment on enjoying it, "Boy, this red wine tastes lovely with my steak." You don't have to forgo your wine or your beer, but be aware of how you refer to *why* you drink. Kids really do take everything in, and if they think wine makes you feel better, they will think it can make them feel better when they don't feel so good.

Peer pressure. Peer pressure comes back to self-esteem. The more self-esteem and confidence your daughter has, the less likely she will give in to peer pressure. Ask her about her friends. Does she feel like she can be herself around them? Is she afraid to be herself because she doesn't want them to make fun of her? Encourage her to be herself and find friends who appreciate her for who she is. Perhaps the person who said it best is Dr. Seuss, "Be who you are and say what you feel, because those who mind don't matter, and those who matter don't mind." Give her a mantra like that to think about and work with her, and maybe even a counselor on building her confidence.

Boredom. She is bored with her friends. She might be bored all the time. This is one of the big signs of depression. Boredom with everything. Nothing feels exciting. When kids are looking for ways to spice things up, drugs and alcohol are easy to find. Help her find ways to have fun. Maybe she needs a new social circle, a new activity, or maybe she just needs a break from the same old, same old. Help her find new activities and inspiration.

Identifying why your daughter is drinking can help you and your daughter identify strategies to help her stop drinking.

Action 9: Listen to what your daughter tells you and help her pinpoint the reasons she feels she needs to drink or use drugs. Help her deal with these issues.

What if you have tried all of this and she is still drinking or using? You need to do everything you can to get her to stop. Definitely seek outside help if you haven't already. It can be very scary if she needs to go to a hospital or treatment center, but it's a heck of a lot less scary than if she ends up really hurting herself by drinking too much or using too many drugs. We look at experimentation as part of growing up, when really, it doesn't have to be that way. Some kids might try a beer and think it is gross and that is the end of that. Some kids try a beer and think it is gross but keep drinking because it is cool. And some kids try a beer and think it is the answer to all their troubles. You never know, and kids never know, how dangerous a beer may be for them. Educate your child, keep talking, work hard on keeping communication open, and view any type of alcohol or drug use as very serious.

Action 10: Seek help when you need it and do everything in your power to keep your daughter sober.

Chapter 12:
Action Recap

Action 1: Mentally prepare and brush up on drug and alcohol trends to ready yourself to have a conversation about drugs and alcohol with your daughter.

Action 2: Have a conversation with your daughter that is educational, nonjudgmental, punishment free, allows her to ask questions, and sets out future expectations and rules.

Action 3: Don't forget to include prescription, over-the-counter medicines, and tobacco products in your conversations.

Action 4: Keep the conversations about alcohol and drugs going.

Action 5: Be a good role model, and surround her with other positive role models.

Action 6: Teach her how to entertain herself and make sure she has options other than drugs and alcohol.

Action 7: Get to know the warning signs of drug and alcohol use, but don't drive yourself nuts looking for what isn't there. When in doubt, take a trip to her primary care physician.

Action 8: Have a conversation or several conversations with her about her use if you find out that she is using. Make sure that she is sober, don't yell, ask why she is using, and follow through on consequences.

Action 9: Listen to what your daughter tells you and help her pinpoint the reasons she feels she needs to drink or use drugs. Help her deal with these issues.

Action 10: Seek help when you need it and do everything in your power to keep your daughter sober.

Chapter 12:
Top Five Talking Points

1. I know having big talks with me isn't your idea of fun, so let's have a little one about drugs and alcohol. First off, I want this to be a topic you feel comfortable talking about and not something you have to hide from me. Let's start off in a punishment-free zone. You can tell me anything today and there will be no punishment for it. We can talk about expectations and rules and all that fun stuff later.

2. What do you know about alcohol and drugs? Do you know anyone in school or in the neighborhood who has tried drugs or alcohol?

3. How do you think I feel about drugs and alcohol?

4. Why would you or do you use drugs or alcohol?

5. All it takes is one night of being drunk or high and so much damage can be done that can't always be fixed—damage to your physical body, your emotional well-being, and your relationships.

Chapter 12: *Resources*

General

http://www.acde.org

This is the American Council for Drug Education's website and is chock-full of information.

http://www.getsmartaboutdrugs.com/

This is the Drug Enforcement Administration's website for parents. It has everything you need to know, as well as the latest research and trends.

http://kidshealth.org/kid/grow/drugs_alcohol/know_drugs.html

This entire website is great, but the section on drugs and alcohol explains drugs in kid-friendly terms.

http://www.theantidrug.com/

A great, very comprehensive website about all the drugs out there, how to talk to your teen about drugs, how to know if your teen is using drugs, resources, and advice.

http://www.dare.com/home/default.asp

The DARE acronym stands for Drug Abuse Resistance Education and it is a program that goes into schools and camps and teaches kids about drugs and how to say "no." There is a section of the site for kids only, which has fun games and facts, and a section for parents.

http://www.samhsa.gov

This is a government agency website from the Substance Abuse and Mental Health Services Administration. It has research, information, and resources for everything out there. It can be a bit overwhelming, but if you are looking for statistics or the most up-to-date information on a drug, this is a great place to look.

http://pbskids.org/itsmylife/body/drugabuse/

This is part of PBS's website and it is a great resource to look at with your child. It has information about every major drug and how it affects the body. There is also a rumor and myth section that is quite helpful.

http://www.drugabuse.gov

This is the National Institute on Drug Abuse's website and it has many facts on every drug out there. This one is information dense and you could look at it all day!

Specific Drugs

http://www.inhalants.org/index.htm

This includes everything you need to know about the dangers of inhalants and describes all the different kinds of inhalants that are out there.

http://www.niaaa.nih.gov/

This is the National Institutes of Health's National Institute on Alcohol Abuse and Alcoholism's website. It has a section titled "Alcohol Alert" which is a quick read and very informative with regard to alcohol.

http://www.underagedrinking.samhsa.gov/default.aspx

This is part of SAMHSA, and it is a fantastic resource that focuses on alcohol but really is helpful across the board.

http://www.aacap.org/cs/root/facts_for_families/tobacco_and_kids

This informative fact page is from the American Academy of Child and Adolescent Psychiatry.

http://www.cancer.org/docroot/PED/content/PED_10_2X_Child_and
_Teen_Tobacco_Use.asp?sitearea=PED

This is the American Cancer Society's information page about kids and tobacco. It is worth a look because it describes different types of tobacco and nicknames, as well as statistics and resources on how to quit.

THIRTEEN

All About the Benjamins

"She really deserved those sneakers. I just couldn't help myself. It isn't like *she* went without food, and I didn't tell her that I wasn't eating. I would tell her that I had a stomachache or that I had already eaten. It was worth it to go without eating for a few weeks to see the look on her face when I gave her those sneakers. Now she has what the other kids have. It isn't her fault that I lost my job."

At this check-in meeting, Mom was coming clean about how difficult things had been since she lost her job. As soon as Mom came into the picture, it was clear that something had drastically changed in her life. Mom, once vibrant and bubbly, looked exhausted, drawn, and sad. Gabby, her ten-year-old, was dressed to the nines all the time. She had all the new clothes, a cool backpack, and the best sneakers. But if you knew her, you would know that something wasn't quite right. Gabby confessed, "I think something is going on with my mom—like she is sick or something. She never eats anymore, and she seems really stressed out. I saw her put her favorite pretzels back on the shelf at the grocery store yesterday, but then she bought me an extra pack of the cookies I like to bring to school with me. Do you know if she is sick? Can you tell me?"

This concern prompted an individual meeting with Mom to find out what was going on, and then a meeting with Gabby to explain what was actually going on. Mom definitely felt relieved getting their financial difficulties off her chest, and Gabby was overjoyed that the only problem was money—not Mom's health. Kids are savvier than we often realize when it comes to who has what, who *doesn't* have certain things, how they stack up against everyone else, and whether money is a struggle or not. It is important to teach kids early on about money and how to use it and save it, so they can be smart with money as they get older.

Action 1: Recognize that your daughter is aware of who has money and who doesn't.

PERSONAL FINANCES

No matter what your financial situation, it is important to teach your daughter about money. It often seems as though money is the elephant in the room, a dirty secret, or a taboo. People who flaunt it are obnoxious; people who don't have it are pitied. Yet so many people struggle with money. Maybe not as many people would struggle with money if they were taught how to manage it well from an early age.

Do you know how to manage money well? Is money something that is hard for you to manage? Does one partner handle the money, while the other has no idea what is going on? Do you keep secrets from your partner about how much money you spend? Do you argue about money? Do you tell your daughter that your partner has a spending problem and shouldn't be allowed to have a debit card?

You might not even be aware of how you talk about money, how you save money, or how you spend money. So definitely take a peek at your own spending, how money is discussed at home, and how you and everyone else in the household handle money. Be honest about money. Money is scary, but it is better to face money difficulties than to hide from them.

Get your own money situation settled. It is hard to teach great habits to your daughter and be taken seriously if your own finances are a mess.

Action 2: Look at your own money habits. Face your finances and fix anything that is out of whack.

Do you practice what you preach? Are you constantly telling your daughter that she spends frivolously, while often lugging in shopping bags from the local department store? Do you tell your daughter that she needs to save, while failing to set aside any of your own money? She is going to figure it out and call you out on it. If your intention is to teach her to save and to encourage better habits than your own, that is noble; however, kids really learn by example. If she sees you getting away with not saving, she is going to think she can, too. If you recognize some trouble areas for yourself, why not work on those? You could even have her help you!

Action 3: Practice positive money habits so your daughter can learn by example.

Wait a minute . . . have your daughter help you? Absolutely! This is one of the best ways to teach kids about money. Make it a game. How many coupons can we find for the grocery store? How many nickels can we save in a month? What fun activities that don't cost money can we do as a family? Educate your daughter while you participate in things. Let her know that if she goes to a movie on Friday night, then she will have to wait until the following week to go mini-golfing since going to a movie is expensive. Teach her how you choose items or events for which to save or spend. For example, tell her that you buy generic cereals so you can save a little there and spend more on organic produce. Helping her learn your everyday spending habits will help her develop her own. Teach her any systems that you have that have worked for you in the past, and warn her about any slip ups that you have made.

Action 4: Involve your daughter in day-to-day money decisions.

Another helpful way to introduce your daughter to money is to help her set goals. Maybe she has a paper route, a babysitting job, or can make money doing chores around the house. Talk to her about what she would like to do with her money. For example, she may tell you, "I would really like to buy a new pair of leggings." Ask her the following questions:

"How much do they cost?"

"When would you like to have the money ready to purchase them?"

"How much are you making every week?"

Based on her answers, help her figure out how much money she needs to set aside each week, or each month, to save the right amount by the date she would like to purchase the leggings. You can also suggest that she put the money she is saving in a space that is separate from any other money she has so that it is physically set aside for her purchase.

If your daughter isn't earning enough money to save for her purchase in a timely fashion, consider lending her the money and having her pay you back on a payment plan. You might even give her handmade promissory notes and write out a payment plan. Make it fun so that it isn't too overwhelming and so that she learns from it. Teaching her how to manage money is really one of the best things you can do for your daughter.

As far as what she wants to buy and why she wants to buy it, you will have to step in at times; at other times, you will have to bite your tongue. If she is spending frivolously, you might have to take control over her finances for a period of time to make sure that she is saving and putting money toward things that she is responsible for buying. You can hold the money for her, or better yet, bring her to the bank to deposit a percentage of her money into a savings account. It is okay for her to make some small financial mistakes. For example, if you know that she is saving for leggings, and she goes out and buys two new nail polishes, you can certainly point out to her that the four dollars she just spent on nail polish would have helped her reach her leggings goal a week sooner. She might discover that it was a mistake to buy the nail polish and think twice the next time she considers spending money.

Action 5: Help your daughter set her own goals in terms of spending and saving.

Does your daughter have a bank account where she can save money? Does she use a debit card? Research the banks around you and see if any have programs for kids. There are some great ones out there that even have incentives to help people save. When she is really young, holding on to money for her is fine, but as she gets older, she needs to learn responsibility such as balancing her bank account, checking her balance, understanding interest, and understanding saving in general. So many people are financially ignorant, either due to denial or simply not understanding the financial system. If you don't understand your own finances, have someone at the bank help you explain different terms to her in a way that both she and you will understand.

Action 6: Open a bank account for your daughter.

FAMILY FINANCES

How much should she know about the family finances? She probably knows more than you realize. Like Gabby, your daughter likely sees when you hold back on buying things and when you are savvy about clipping coupons. Does she need to know that you literally used the nineteen cents you found under the seat in your car to come up with the remainder of her lunch money for the week? No. There's no need to freak her out. Can you let her know that times are tough, and everyone needs to prioritize which items are necessities and which are indulgences? Absolutely. Letting her know that spending needs to slow down for a while can help her to appreciate your financial obligations.

As much as kids notice when times are tough, they also recognize an extra night out, a new couch, a vacation, or any other money spent above and beyond the usual. Perhaps you saved for it, maybe you got a raise or a bonus, or maybe you decided to spend more than usual just because. Whatever the case, use it as a way to demonstrate appropriate spending. Just because you are treating your family to something more expensive than usual doesn't mean it is going to continue. Spending frivolously on a continual basis won't teach your daughter anything helpful in terms of spending and saving. In times when money is not an issue, it is still important to teach your daughter how to spend and save smartly!

Action 7: Be honest about the family finances, and use changes in finances as a way to educate your daughter about money.

MONEY WOES

Most people will face a financial blow of some sort in their lives. It could come by way of a job loss, poor saving, overwhelming debt, illness, death of a financial contributor, or in many other ways. Sometimes the loss doesn't seem dramatic, and life as usual can continue with a few changes here and there. Unfortunately, big money issues tend to be noticeable to others and could cause stress to your daughter. If your house is foreclosed on, if you lose your job and are unemployed, if your car is repossessed, or if your daughter can no longer participate in after-school activities that cost money—all of these are big signals to your daughter that you have taken a substantial financial blow.

How you handle it will help your daughter deal with any stress she may feel over the change. If you can be as focused as possible on the great things you do have, such as your health, your family, happiness, and so on, you will set a great example for your daughter about what really matters. It sounds totally lame, and probably will to your daughter, but it really is true that money can't buy happiness. Point out that all of the money in the world couldn't buy the excitement of the moment you shared with your daughter when she did her first headstand. You are going to need to be creative. It will be easier with younger girls because they will believe you more than teenagers will. It will also be much easier if you didn't have much money to begin with, and there is little obvious change occurring. But even the most cynical daughter, who really wants the cool handbag that *everyone* has, can be shown that life is not all about money. Can money make things easier? Yes, in many cases it can. But does it make or break life? No. Will your family and your daughter need to make sacrifices? Probably. Money or lack of money can even affect huge, life-changing decisions such as where she goes to high school or college. Life is what you make of it. There are so many ways to have fun and enjoy life without spending money. You need to show her those ways.

What about her friends? What if their families are all doing well financially and she is suddenly unable to afford the things she used to do with them? This is where money woes will probably impact your daughter the most. If you handle it in stride, this will help her handle it well, too. It isn't something she should be embarrassed about, and if kids are being mean to her about it, or if friends have dropped her due to her change in economic status, they are pretty crummy friends. It could mean that you need to get involved and make sure that any negative comments stop. If your house was foreclosed on, if something public happened that to many would seem humiliating, try to help her understand that this is nothing *she* caused. The amount of money, the money mistakes, the loss of money, or the loss of economic status, does not change the person she is, and it is not a reflection of her ability to handle money. It doesn't change who you are; it doesn't change who your family is. Those who love your daughter for being a great kid will continue to do so with or without money. In times of financial distress, really good friends will stick by you and your family.

> On the JumpStart Coalition for Personal Financial Literacy's website, it says, "the average student who graduates from high school lacks basic skills in the management of personal financial affairs. Many are unable to balance a checkbook and most simply have no insight into the basic survival principles involved with earning, spending, saving and investing." Yikes!! Let's get our girls the financial education they need!

Your daughter may notice things that you may find trivial when dealing with a public loss of money. The bag she can't afford may become an obsession, and she may bad-mouth you for not buying it for her. She is probably angry that something completely out of her control is impacting her life. She might also be embarrassed by you or your partner if one of you lost your job or your house. Your loss of money becomes her burden to carry even if you tell her not to worry about it. If she is embarrassed or ashamed, she might act angry with you for screwing up her life. Did you do it on purpose? No. Explain that to her. It is so tough to explain that money, something completely out of her power, can impact who her friends are, where she gets her education, and the activities in which she can participate. Help her deal with her anger. It is okay for her to be angry with you for a bit. If you lost your job, she might also be angry at the place that laid you off. This is okay.

Let her work through her anger. Talk to her about it. Let her grieve the life she had before. And remind her, this is temporary. Finances change, people get new jobs, and people buy new homes. Don't let her experience anger or sadness over the change in status. You need to move on and so does she. It is a tough lesson to learn, but it could actually motivate her to learn about finances, how to protect herself in the future, and the importance of saving. Stay positive and ask for help from those around you. Don't be ashamed and teach her that she shouldn't be ashamed either. Regardless of whether her family is rich, poor, middle class, or anything in between, she is the same wonderful person she has always been.

Action 8: Teach her that she is not defined by the amount of money her family does or does not have. A loss of financial status can be really tough, but it is not the end of the world.

What if you come into a large amount of money: You win the lottery, you sell a screenplay, or something changes your economic status in the other direction? Isn't that a money boon? Not always. Now you need to make sure that you don't start spending excessively. Money can come and go. Teach your daughter that having money does not change who *she* is. There is no reason to switch friends, buy insanely expensive handbags, or act like a snob. Just like not having money wasn't her fault, having money isn't either. Try to stay away from giving her money whenever she wants it just because you can. Nothing should really change for her; she still needs to appreciate the value of money and how to save and prioritize it when she spends.

Change as little as possible. Don't flaunt your new money; it will only set a bad example. "Friends" will come out of the woodwork. If you publicly came into more money, suggest that she brush off comments about money. It isn't anyone's business. No matter how much money your family has, she should never feel like she has to share how much money your family has, how many houses you own, or anything else related to socioeconomic status.

Having money may make certain things easier. She might not need to stress over where she goes to high school, or if she can afford to take dance lessons or other such activities. Teach her that this isn't so for everyone. Make sure that she doesn't judge others based on their family's finances.

Action 9: She is not defined by money, so why talk about it? Encourage her to keep the family finances a family matter.

Teach her how to handle money well. Don't spend above your means to buy her frivolous things. She doesn't need a designer handbag as badly as she or even you might think she does. The best gift to give your daughter is an understanding of how to manage money, and how to not let it define who she is. With or without a designer bag, she is still the same great kid.

Chapter 13:
Action Recap

Action 1: Recognize that your daughter is aware of who has money and who doesn't.

Action 2: Look at your own money habits. Face your finances and fix anything that is out of whack.

Action 3: Practice positive money habits so your daughter can learn by example.

Action 4: Involve your daughter in day-to-day money decisions.

Action 5: Help your daughter set her own goals in terms of spending and saving.

Action 6: Open a bank account for your daughter.

Action 7: Be honest about the family finances, and use changes in finances as a way to educate your daughter about money.

Action 8: Teach her that she is not defined by the amount of money she does or does not have. A loss of financial status can be really tough, but it is not the end of the world.

Action 9: She is not defined by money, so why talk about it? Encourage her to keep the family finances a family matter.

Chapter 13:
Top Five Talking Points

1. So I was thinking, maybe we should take a trip to the bank so you can open an account to start saving money. What do you think?

2. It is so important that you learn how to save money and balance your spending and saving. I know saving doesn't seem as much fun as spending, but I bet you will be really proud of yourself if we set a savings goal and you make it!!

3. Everyone has different financial situations. Regardless of anyone's circumstances, having or not having money doesn't make you a better or worse person. If anyone ever tells you any differently, let me know.

4. I know that you are having a difficult time dealing with our losing our house, and I am really sorry about it. It isn't your fault that this is happening, and I know you have to deal with the fallout. I am working really hard to get us back on track. We will all have to sacrifice for a bit, but we will be okay.

5. I know it seems like money is really important, and it is, but what is most important is our family, our health, our happiness, and our memories of good times together. It sounds really cheesy, but it is really true! All the money in the world couldn't give me as much happiness as I have when I am just spending time with you.

Chapter 13: *Resources*

http://www.usmint.gov/kids/Teachers/financialLiteracy/
This is a fun part of the United States Mint's website. It has lesson plans for teachers and fun resources for parents. http://www.jumpstart.org/ The goal of this group is to provide financial education resources for all students K–12. It has cool teaching tips you can use with your daughter and links to helpful websites.

http://www.themint.org/
This interactive website has fun for kids, tips for teens, and resources for parents and teachers.

http://www.childrensfinancialnetwork.com/
This website is also fun and interactive. It is definitely kid-friendly, and parent-friendly, too!

http://www.countrybankforkids.com/
This is an impressive look at what a bank can do for your child. Look into programs like this at banks close to you. The bank works with teachers and parents to teach kids about money.

FOURTEEN

Parental Stress

Jason and Pam were thinking about separating, but they didn't think that they should tell Sarah, their daughter, about it since she was only eight years old. "We decided to tell her that Jason has to travel for business every week and that he'll just stay at our house on the weekends. We can pretend to go to bed together. Then, once Sarah is asleep, Jason will go downstairs and sleep on the couch. We don't want her worrying in case we don't end up divorcing."

Jason and Pam meant well; they really wanted to protect their daughter from stress and pain. However, Sarah was already aware that something was going on, and the secrecy and unpredictability of it all was driving her crazy.

Sarah explained, "I know my mom and dad are probably getting divorced. They yell at each other all the time. But then sometimes they hug and snuggle on the couch, so sometimes I think they aren't going to get divorced. I was pretty sure they were getting divorced yesterday because my dad tried to hug my mom, but she wouldn't hug him back."

"Did they tell you anything about divorce?"

"No, but Tabitha, the girl in my class with the red hair, said that her parents fought a lot before they got divorced and her dad slept on the couch just like my dad does."

"Are you worried about your parents getting divorced?"

"Sometimes. But I think if they got divorced and lived in different houses, they wouldn't fight so much and that would be better."

Sarah's parents were very surprised to hear that she had been doing some investigating with her peers about what it means when Dad sleeps on the couch and both parents yell a lot. They also didn't realize that she had heard so much of what they were saying to one another, and how much she noticed about their body language. What seemed to be bothering Sarah most was that they didn't talk to her about what was going on, so she was guessing all the time. This was making her very anxious. Could her parents have completely spared her any anxiety? No, but they could certainly have worked to lessen her anxiety by talking to Sarah about what was going on instead of trying to hide it.

Kids usually know when something is going on with their parents. They notice when a door slams, when a kiss is avoided, when they are hugged more tightly than usual, or when someone is distracted. As they get older, they notice even more and can often figure out even more. Parents can get away with hiding things up until about the time their children are about age four or five; after that, parents should probably discuss with their child any stress they are experiencing. Of course, how they should address it will depend on the age and maturity of their child and how much it will directly affect her. More often than not, addressing parental stress in some way is more helpful than some ridiculous cover-up or pretending as though everything is just fine.

Action 1: Hiding parental stress from your daughter is probably not a good idea. Addressing the situation with her may cause less stress for everyone.

Divorce is a subject that causes stress for everyone in the household. This must be addressed eventually if that is what is happening in your family. There are other times, however, that you or your partner might be stressed out and it could have little or nothing at all to do with the rest of the household. Perhaps you are having a particularly tough time at work, or you are anxious about a friend who is ill. Other sources of stress that could more directly impact your household might include the death or illness of someone in the family, a job loss or change, a move, financial difficulties, or legal trouble. When parents are stressed, the whole family does feel it.

So what are you supposed to do? Never feel stress? Hide it? Stress is inevitable. You are going to have it and so is your daughter. You cannot protect her from stress, but you can teach her, by example, how to cope with stress. If you show your feelings, showing her the resolution to the stress can teach her that things can get better or resolve. If the end result is negative, she will also learn that despite the negative outcome, life still goes on and there are ways to manage.

In the book *NurtureShock,* the authors include interesting research by Dr. E. Mark Cummings. He found that children who witness an argument between their parents and then witness a sincere resolution are generally okay with the argument. It is the kids who only see half the argument or no arguing at all who miss out on a lesson in conflict resolution. Witnessing the resolution also created less aggressive reactions from children who had witnessed an argument.

Instead of hiding our anger or stress, it is important to show it (appropriately) and then show how we manage it. This is the only way our kids will learn how to handle their anger, stress, and anxieties. If we spend our time hiding emotions, dealing with anger by punching walls, faking our calm, cool, and collectedness, we are doing our kids a huge disservice. They need to learn from us, and there is no learning going on if we hide everything.

Action 2: Show your emotions and the resolution to those emotions so your daughter can learn how to deal with her own stressors, anxieties, and anger.

Show your emotions—within reason. If you are so stressed out that you are going to physically hurt someone or you are afraid you can't handle the emotions you are feeling, you need to get some help. Reaching out for help is another positive way of showing your daughter how to manage emotions. She will know that if she is feeling overwhelmed, it is okay for her to reach out for help as well. There is no shame in doing this. If you are seriously at a breaking point, and your stress has you not eating, punching walls, screaming profanities at your partner, or feeling as though you cannot think straight, you need to step back and seek counseling or help of some sort. Watching you manage your emotions in a negative way is also teaching your daughter negative coping skills. If your emotions are out of control, get some help.

Action 3: If you cannot handle your emotions, seek help so you can continue to be a positive role model for your daughter.

Let's look at Sarah again. Her parents did hide some aspects of their stress, but they also showed some of it, too.

"I don't like when my mom talks to my dad all cranky. And then they fight sometimes and I don't like that either. I get really sad when they call each other names."

"It is normal for people to argue, Sarah, even though I know you don't like to hear it. What happens after they argue?"

"Dad usually says sorry to Mom and then Mom says she is sorry, too."

"So does that make you feel better?"

"Kind of, but I am still mad at them."

"Why? If they aren't mad at each other anymore and you know they apologized to each other, what are you still mad about?"

"I get really upset when they yell and scream."

"Do you believe that they are sorry?"

"To each other! But no one ever says they are sorry to me and I am the one who is scared!!"

When Mom and Dad heard this, they were shocked! It had never occurred to them that they should apologize to their daughter for arguing. They had been so good about letting Sarah know that all adults argue, and then they apologize to one another and things are okay, but they didn't realize that she might be pretty mad at them for their behavior. From then on, they apologized to her when she heard them call each other names or say mean things to one another. It made her feel heard and respected, and it made a huge difference in how she was feeling.

Your behavior toward your partner or anyone else in the home may affect your daughter in ways that you might not even realize. Everyone was so worried about Sarah being stressed or sad, that no one really thought of her feeling angry. When she was asked, she was pretty quick to let them know how angry she was. She had every right to be angry. She wasn't angry about the arguing itself, but the way they argued scared her, and hearing them apologize to each other and then not to her only made her angrier. To her parents, it was as if she was watching them from the outside, when to her, she was part of it. Appreciate that your daughter may be in a similar situation. Maybe you have been really stressed about work and assume that your daughter is angry that you haven't been able to make it home for dinner in a week. Perhaps she isn't angry at all, but instead is worried about you and needs some reassurance that you are managing the stress fine and that it will be over soon.

Action 4: Ask your daughter how she feels about the stress she is witnessing. Don't just assume she is feeling a certain way; you could be totally wrong.

How do you know what to tell her about your stress? Aren't some things "adult stuff"? Yes. Some things are actually better left unsaid, but you still have to address the fact that you or your partner or both are feeling stress. Details are generally unnecessary, and quite often you just need to tell your daughter, "Hey, I know I have been a bit preoccupied lately, and I am really sorry. There are some things at work going on that have me super stressed out. I think most of it will be over within the next couple of weeks, so if you can bear with me until then, that would be great!"

When it comes to an illness in the family or an illness in the home, it is important to be as informed as you possibly can be before reacting or talking to your daughter about the particulars of the illness. For example, if you hear that your aunt is gravely ill and she only has three days to live, verify everything before talking to your daughter. Letting her know that your aunt is sick and that you are worried about her could be enough. If it is you that is ill, it is also important to wait until you know the severity of your illness before giving too many details. If you can avoid scaring her unnecessarily, that is great. You might be scared yourself, but if you can pull yourself together so you don't freak your daughter out, that would be helpful. This is also an opportunity for a teachable moment in how to calmly deal with stress.

Before talking to her about what is stressing you out, make sure that you are in the right mind-set to talk about it. If you are talking to her with your husband about your potential divorce, try and get any anger or tears out ahead of time. If either one of you falls apart during the conversation, she is going to have a hard time believing that things will really be okay. Plan out the conversation. If you are talking to her alone, it may be a bit easier to plan the conversation. If you and your partner are speaking to her together, make sure that you are on the same page about what to tell her. Assure her that you love her, and will continue to love her. Make sure you know who will take care of her, because she is likely to ask about this. For instance, if you are sick and will be out of commission for a while, figure out who will be there to step in. Who will take her to school? Who will pack her lunch? How long will that person stay with her? This is one of the reasons it is a good idea to plan ahead. Try and think of questions and concerns she might have ahead of time and figure out the answers.

Action 5: Prepare yourself and what you will say prior to talking to your daughter so that you know what you want to get across to her and so that she knows that she will be loved and taken care of.

We will all face stress at some point. Hopefully, it will not last long, and our daughters will come through stronger than they were before. This chapter is meant to give a general overview on how to handle parental stress. If you have a big issue to deal with like the death of a parent, a serious illness, or a divorce, there are many great resources that speak specifically to those circumstances. Please see the resource section at the end of this chapter for some of these big issues.

Chapter 14:
Action Recap

Action 1: Hiding parental stress from your daughter is probably not a good idea. Addressing the situation with her may cause less stress for everyone.

Action 2: Show your emotions and the resolutions to those emotions so your daughter can learn how to deal with her own stressors, anxieties, and anger.

Action 3: If you cannot handle your emotions, seek help so you can continue to be a positive role model for your daughter.

Action 4: Ask your daughter how she feels about the stress she is witnessing. Don't just assume she is feeling a certain way; you could be totally wrong.

Action 5: Prepare yourself and what you will say prior to talking to your daughter so that you know what you want to get across to her and so that she knows that she will be loved and taken care of.

Chapter 14:
Top Five Talking Points

1. I was thinking that you might have noticed I am a little preoccupied lately. I am dealing with some stress, and sometimes I just get spaced out. I am sorry if it is affecting you. I am trying really hard to manage the stress and I think I am doing okay, but if you see me spacing out too much, just let me know!!

2. I know we talked about the stress I am under right now. I was just wondering if it is bothering you. If it is, how is it making you feel?

3. Crying, being angry, or being tired; these are all normal ways that stress can affect you. But lately, I feel like I have been even more upset than that, so I am going to talk to someone who can help me manage the stress I am feeling.

4. What kinds of things stress you out? I know you know that dirty dishes in the sink stress me out. What bothers you?

5. I am sure that you are feeling pretty stressed about what is going on, but I want you to know that worrying about all of this isn't your job; it is mine. And I am fine with that. I love you very much, and no amount of stress will change my love for you.

Resources for *Specific Stressors*

Divorce

http://kidshealth.org/parent/positive/talk/help_child_divorce.html
This website has great resources on how to talk to kids about divorce and
what reactions to expect from them.

http://helpguide.org/mental/children_divorce.htm
This website includes a great article that discusses the importance of parents taking care of themselves while this is going on so that they can be
the best caretakers possible for their kids.

Illness

**http://www.cancer.org/docroot/CRI/content/CRI_2_6X_Dealing_
With_Diagnosis.asp**
This webpage is mainly about a parent with a cancer diagnosis, but its
advice can be applied to any person a child cares about who is experiencing any type of illness. There is also a link for resources if your child
has cancer.

Death

http://www.cc.nih.gov/ccc/patient_education/pepubs/childeath.pdf
This is the National Institutes of Health's handout for children dealing with
death, and it really covers all the bases. It is very thorough and could be
helpful to adults as well as to children.

FIFTEEN

Transitions

"My neighbor told me that when I move up to middle school, I will only have friends if I date an eighth-grader. I don't even know any eighth-graders. I think the boy on the next street over might be one, but he is big and scary—and definitely not friendly."

"My sister told me that when we move to our new house, I am not going to have any friends and people are going to call me the *new girl*. I don't want to be the new girl. I want to stay here and just be me. I hate my parents."

"My big brother is leaving for college and everyone is so happy for him. They keep telling him how much fun college is going to be. My aunt told me that his leaving will be good for me, too, because I will get more attention. I don't like it, though. I don't want him to go. He is funny, and he is the only one I can talk to about my friends when they are acting stupid."

As if girls didn't have enough transitions already going on within their bodies, many transitions outside of their bodies also occur during these difficult times. They will experience some of these transitions at the same time as their peers, such as transitioning to the middle school or high school. Some transitions, such as moving to a new town, will be experienced solo. Regardless of the transition, it is important for parents to recognize that changes can be challenging for children—even when such changes are generally positive for the child.

There are many steps you can take to help make your daughter's transitions go as smoothly as possible, and signs to look out for to determine whether a change your daughter is experiencing is creating stress for her.

Action 1: Recognize that transitions in your daughter's life, as benign as they might seem, can cause stress and worry.

What constitutes a transition? Any change in your daughter's life. Changes your daughter might experience can be as simple as changing bedrooms at home or as significant as dealing with a death in the family. Changes happen every day, and some girls are more sensitive to changes than others. For some girls, moving to a new school district isn't a big deal; for others, simply driving a different route to school will be upsetting. As a parent, you should try to be aware of changes in your daughter's life that are happening or upcoming. Some are obvious, like moving up to a new and more competitive bracket in softball. But you might not be aware of others unless you remain alert, such as your daughter having to deal with a new math teacher being assigned to her class midyear after the teacher she started out with at the beginning of the year leaves the school.

Anticipating predictable transitions that your daughter will have to face can help you prepare and help your daughter prepare for any emotions she might be feeling. Sometimes, the change could seem so miniscule to both you and your daughter that you might not expect it to be anything more than a small bump in the road; however, often even the tiniest of bumps can throw everything out of alignment. Converse with your daughter, listen to what she has to say, pay close attention to her patterns of behavior, and pick up on any shifts in her usual patterns.

Action 2: Be aware of what transitions are occurring or will soon occur in your daughter's life.

You probably know by now how well your daughter tends to handle change. Is she someone who can roll with the punches, or does she tend to be more rigid and to struggle when things don't go according to her plan or expectation? If your daughter can roll with the punches, great! But that doesn't mean she always will. As she goes through puberty, and must deal with the transitions and stressors in her life, you might find that she isn't as easygoing as she used to be. This doesn't mean she won't adjust well; it may just mean that she will need you to be patient because she may take a little bit longer than usual to adjust to some changes. She might continue to be easygoing and to just roll with things as they happen, or she might act a bit stressed over whatever changes she faces. Be prepared for whatever reaction occurs.

If your daughter is rigid, and has always had difficulty transitioning, all is not lost! She might react just fine to some changes. If her pattern in dealing with change is to experience difficulty or to be always on edge, try not to get caught up in the drama. Prepare for the worst just in case, but don't project onto her that you *know* she is going to react poorly. Maybe she'll surprise you and a change will go more smoothly than you could ever have imagined it would. But if you expect her to have difficulty, and talk with her about whatever change is happening or upcoming in a way that shows you expect it to be difficult for her, this might be a self-fulfilling prophecy. She might experience greater difficulty than she might have experienced had you not projected your anxiety onto her.

Keep in mind that different changes can cause different emotions to bubble to the surface. She might be so excited to get out of middle school that high school seems like the light at the end of the tunnel instead of a daunting transition; as a consequence, the transition might go smoothly. Prepare for a rocky transition just in case, but give her the opportunity to have a great transition. Hold back before assuming gloom and doom. You could be pleasantly surprised.

Certainly use her track record with change as a base, but don't be surprised if it changes.

Action 3: Figure out how your daughter deals with change and allow her the space to handle change with ease or with some difficulty.

Don't project how you think your daughter will react or how you think she should react. Don't say things like, "Cindy is never going to adjust to our new house; she can't stand any change to her routines!" or, "Caroline won't mind if we move her bedroom to the basement; she is so easygoing." Projecting your thoughts onto your daughter will cause you to treat her with kid gloves when she doesn't need them, or to potentially walk all over her just because she is so laid back.

If you say things to your daughter that suggest that you think she won't be able to handle a change, she might believe you and handle it poorly. Had you just let her experience the change without freaking out about it, she may have been just fine. On the other hand, saying things to your daughter like, "Oh, it will be fine; you are always fine" could invalidate how she might be feeling. Maybe she isn't fine this time. Keep an open mind about any emotions she might be experiencing. If she doesn't react as she usually does, you might ask her about it in an observational way. Don't say, "You should be nervous about this; this is a huge change!" That will only make her nervous, when perhaps she was handling the transition pretty calmly up until then.

Action 4: Don't project onto her how you think she should react or will react. Let her reaction happen on its own.

How can you best prepare for the detours your daughter's life will take? Support her, listen to her, and help her adjust. In terms of transitions you know are coming, prepare her for leaving one chapter of her life and starting another. For example, if she is making the move to high school, celebrate her leaving middle school. What a success she has been!! Congratulate her for getting through such a tough part of her life. Talk to her about the high school. Prepare her for the change. What about the change worries her? What about the change excites her? If you have an opportunity to visit the school, do so. Work with other parents you know to support the group of children who are going through the same transition. Find out what would make her first week less stressful, how she would like to get to school (have her practice her route), who she would like to commute to school with, and any other things you can think of that might help things go smoothly during the transition period. During her first few months of high school, check in with her frequently. Is there anything about middle school that she misses? Is there a way to re-create that in her high school? Listen to what she has to say.

It is speculated that the Chinese symbol for the word "crisis" came from "danger" plus "opportunity." If you look at change as scary but intriguing, daunting but with a potential for opportunity, you open yourself up to its possibilities. Encourage your daughter to view change in this way. You can demonstrate to her how to make the best of things by showing her that you do this in your own life.

What if she experiences a sudden change? Does this change involve just loss, or does it also offer potential gain? Help her see any bright side the change may offer. Is there a silver lining to it? Is there a way to make lemonade out of lemons? Maybe there is. Some transitions seem to be negative all around, no matter how you look at the change. If this is the case, continue to listen to her and to hear her out. Is there a way to make it better once it has happened? Is there a way to go back? Does she just need to adjust before she realizes that things aren't that bad?

Action 5: Support her through transitions by preparing her as much as you can, listening to her fears, and helping her find a bright side to the transitions if there is one.

What should you be on the lookout for with respect to change and your daughter? Any change in your daughter's behavior can be significant. Has middle school started, but her sleep is now fitful? Ask her about it. You might find that she is sleeping fitfully because she is texting all night long and not really trying to sleep; or you could find that she genuinely hasn't been able to sleep well since school started. Sleep, eating habits, motivation, energy level, mood, patterns of behavior, and relationships are all key things to keep tabs on in terms of how your daughter is feeling about any changes in her life.

If you notice changes, point them out in a nice way. You might say, "Heather, since you moved up to the middle school, you don't seem to be as active as you were in elementary school. Is everything okay?" Try to avoid accusatory or invalidating comments such as, "Heather, you have been a nightmare since you moved up to middle school. I guess middle school brought on all the horrors of adolescence. I can only imagine how difficult this year is going to be." Encouraging her to accept changes instead of discouraging her with negative chatter is a great way to help her through transitions.

Transitions and changes are occurring everywhere around her, and your daughter could feel as though she doesn't have any control over her life or her body. She has boobs, she is going to middle school for the first time, there is a cutie-pie in her class, her school performance is separating her from her friends, some of her friends have started experimenting with drugs, her favorite dolls are no longer cool to have in her room—all of these things are out of her control. The boobs will grow, schools will change, love interests crop up, academic performance now determines who is in her classes, substance abuse is everywhere, and social pressures to conform become more important to her than her own interests. This is a tough time. With all these changes going on, you could witness your daughter desperately trying to control something in her life so that she feels some sense of power. Unfortunately, in that scramble to find some control, she could develop some pretty detrimental coping skills, such as trying to control her eating to the point that she develops an eating disorder, becoming more rigid about her schedule to the point where she cannot have fun, or engaging in obsessive behaviors. If any of these seem to be troubling your daughter, talk to her about seeing a counselor. Encourage her to talk about things with you, or with another adult with whom she is close. Help her vent her frustrations about not having much control.

Action 6: Be on the lookout for any changes in her behavior or any unhealthy attempts to assert control over her life. Get help for her if it is needed.

Children really don't have much control in their lives. As they age, they want more control and they might resort to some unhealthy behaviors to gain some sort of control. You can help her identify parts of her life where she *does* have control, and that can help immensely. Instead of focusing on everything she doesn't have control over, enlightening her on what she can control in a healthy way can be very helpful.

So what does your daughter have control over? That depends on your household. Maybe she is carted around with you everywhere you go. Now is a good time, if you haven't done so already, to start including her in family decisions. Letting her have a voice on where the family will vacation, what is for dinner on Thursday nights, or what sport she wants to play will give her a sense of inclusion. Just being included in certain decisions can make her feel more in control of her life.

Remind her that she does have control over aspects of her life, such as whom she chooses for friends, how she carries herself, if she is polite, if she is kind, what she does with her body, and who she allows to touch her body. As girls grow up, they don't always recognize all that they do have control over. Many girls seem to think things just *happen* to them, and they don't always see their role in these things. For example, if your daughter really wants to go to a party this weekend, but can't because she hasn't finished her homework, then she has a great deal of control over this situation. If she does her homework, she can go to the party. She might not see it that way; she might see it as not being allowed to go to a party because her mom is mean. However, she is in total control of the situation. Friendly reminders of how your daughter can earn privileges can help remind her of how she can exert more control.

Many times things will be out of her control, but learning how she can respond to these things, or work to change them should help her take control over her life.

Action 7: Help your daughter identify and focus on those aspects of her life over which she does have control.

"My daughter told me yesterday that she hates our new house and she is going back to live with my mother. I don't understand. She seemed fine with the move last year."

Did your family have a transition a while ago that is now your daughter's reason for everything that is wrong with her life? Did the transition seem fine at first, but is now the root of all evil? This is not a rare occurrence. Your daughter could have felt fine about it at first or even been excited about the change, then suddenly starts to look depressed, have trouble sleeping, or become very clingy. She might point to the change in her life as the reason for her mood change, or she might not know why her mood has changed. It could be that she is having a delayed reaction to the transition. Everything that was new and exciting has worn off, and she now has time to miss the things she left. Even if the change really is for the better, she still might need to grieve the past. It is normal to grieve the past even when a change is positive. If she is having a delayed reaction to the transition, this doesn't mean that it will be more difficult to handle; it is just something to be aware of or to think about if she doesn't seem to be as happy as she was before the change took place. For example, if we lose someone, we are often sad initially, and then move on and do okay—until there is some event or anniversary that reminds us of what we miss in the person we lost. This could be what your daughter is experiencing.

If you think your daughter is having a delayed reaction to a change in her life, deal with it like you would if she had just encountered the change by supporting her, listening to her, and pointing out any positive things that have occurred since the transition. Seeing how things have improved or could improve since the transition may be helpful to her.

Action 8: Be prepared for a possible delayed reaction to a transition.

Transitions or change can be tough on everyone. You should reflect on whether the changes your daughter has experienced might be having an effect on you, too.

Chapter 15:
Action Recap

Action 1: Recognize that transitions in your daughter's life, as benign as they might seem, can cause stress and worry.

Action 2: Be aware of what transitions are occurring or will occur in your daughter's life.

Action 3: Figure out how your daughter deals with change and allow her the space to handle change with ease or with some difficulty.

Action 4: Don't project onto her how you think she should react or will react. Let her reaction unfold on its own.

Action 5: Support her through transitions by preparing her as much as you can, listening to her fears, and helping her find a bright side to the transitions if there is one.

Action 6: Be on the lookout for any changes in her behavior or any unhealthy attempts to assert control over her life. Get help for her if it is needed.

Action 7: Help your daughter identify and focus on aspects of her life over which she does have control.

Action 8: Be prepared for a possible delayed reaction to a transition.

Chapter 15:
Top Five Talking Points

1. _____ is a pretty big change for you!
   How are you feeling about it? Do you have any questions or
   concerns? I know change can be scary sometimes, but it can
   also be really fun and exciting!

2. How are you feeling since _____;
   is there anything you would like to discuss?

3. I know a lot of changes in your life seem to happen without
   your input. Your body is changing and your friends are acting
   differently. These kinds of things can be pretty frustrating and
   they might make you feel like a lot of things are out of your
   control. I want you to know that I think what you have to say
   is really important, and that you do have a say in what goes
   on in this family. Sometimes I have to make a decision that
   isn't what you want, but I do listen. I want you to speak up
   more, so you will know that you do have some control over
   what happens in our family.

4. Not only do you have some control over what happens in
   our family, but also you have control over you! The choices
   you make, the way you act toward others, and the amount of
   effort you put into things are all ways you can control how
   your life turns out. You will hit obstacles here and there like
   we all do, but only you are in charge of your life. That is
   why it is so important that you make good choices.

5. I have noticed that you haven't really been yourself lately.
   Is everything okay? I know you (changed schools/stopped
   playing baseball) a while ago, but that could be what is
   bothering you. What do you think?

SIXTEEN

Adults Behaving Badly

"Chrissy's mom is totally fine with us drinking in her basement. I don't know why you are such a bitch about stuff like that.
Now I can't even go over to her house? Thanks a lot. You are going
to ruin my life!"

Yup. You might ruin her life temporarily, but when thoughtless
adults are involved, you have to step in and take care of things.
Letting your daughter fend for herself in situations with unsafe
adults is not fair to her. This is a prime example of when your daughter needs you to be involved even if she doesn't want you to be
involved.

Sarah, the daughter, is spilling the beans on everything that is
happening at Chrissy's house. This means that the behavior doesn't
make her feel safe and she wants protection from it by her mother.
If she didn't, she would just keep it a secret.

Does this mean that she will love her mother dearly and shower
her with thanks when she forbids her from going to Chrissy's house

again? Unfortunately, no it does not mean that. In fact, she might hold it against her mother until she is about thirty years old. Only then might she realize, "Gee, Mom was really looking out for me there. I totally get why she did that now." She still probably won't thank her mother, but she will appreciate the things she did to keep her safe.

Action 1: Listen carefully to what your daughter tells you about the other adults in her life.

As your daughter gets older, she will start to make friends that you won't know. She might hang out after school with kids from her class and stop by the home of one of them. You have less control over whom she hangs out with as she grows up. What you still can do, however, is to try to get to know her friends, find out who lives with them, and keep tabs on where your daughter goes. To do this, you are going to have to keep asking her questions, which will doubtless annoy her and may make her feel suffocated. This is one of those times when you will just have to be persistent in spite of her objections.

There are many ways to successfully coax information from your daughter about a new friend. Here is an example:

"Mom, can I go to Cindy's house after school tomorrow?"

"Isa, is Cindy the new girl in your class?"

"Yes. She is really nice, and she lives right by Uncle Jimmy."

"Why don't you two come here tomorrow instead? We can invite her mom over and welcome her."

Isa rolls her eyes, "Never mind. That would be soooooo embarrassing."

"Her mom might want to meet me. She probably doesn't know many people here. Who else lives with them?"

"Actually, she lives with her aunt. Something happened to her mom. Her brother lives with them, too. He is little, like six or something. Her older cousin lives there, too."

"Isa, I think it might be nice for me to meet her aunt first. It sounds like she has her hands full. What is her number? I can call her and invite her over. I promise I won't embarrass you. If I were her aunt, I would like to get to know my niece's friends. Maybe her aunt and I will hit it off really well, and I will have a new walking buddy!"

Isa reluctantly gives her mom the number. Her mom calls.

Action 2: Ask her about her new friend, where she lives, and who lives with her.

You aren't saying no to your daughter hanging out with her new friend at her friend's house. You just want to get to know the new family before letting your daughter go to their house so that you can be sure that it a safe place for her to go. When Isa was talking to her mother, she mentioned that Cindy and her brother had both moved in with the aunt because their mother wasn't available to take care of them. While it is important to keep an open mind, the mother's absence does raise some questions. Did Cindy lose her mom? Is the aunt overwhelmed? What about the cousin who sleeps there sometimes? Is he in college? Is he in trouble? It is possible that Cindy's mom is unable to care for her kids right now because she is in the midst of cancer treatments and that Cindy's cousin is in college and only lives there during school breaks. Another possibility is that Cindy's mom lost custody of Cindy, the aunt begrudgingly took custody, and the cousin is in and out because he goes in and out of detox programs. Whatever the case, it is up to you to let your daughter know that you want to know the family before you let her go over there, and to then follow through with checking out the family's situation to make sure that your daughter will be safe at their house.

Action 3: Find out from your daughter what her friend's family is like.

Your daughter may have very limited information. It's a good idea to ask her about the family, but it's important to then find out more about them by speaking directly to the friend's parent or guardian.

Call the other parent or guardian and introduce yourself:

"Hi. This is Jen Walters. My daughter, Isa, is in Cindy's class. May I speak to Cindy's aunt, please?"

"This is Cindy's aunt."

"Hi. The girls would really like to get together, and I'd like to invite you and your niece to come over tomorrow so we could meet. I really like to know the families of my daughter's friends.

Isa said you have a little one and an older one as well. They are more than welcome to join us."

"That sounds great! I will definitely bring my little nephew, but you don't want my son coming—trust me."

It's great that the aunt is willing to come over, so you will have an opportunity to get to know her and the two siblings. You won't get to meet the cousin this time, but you might be able to find a way to ask the aunt about her son. What the aunt said is a little concerning, so you really need to make sure that you know everyone who might be in the house before you let your daughter go over there. If her son is in and out of trouble, it would be helpful to know when he is around and when he is away. It might be a good idea to have the girls meet only at your house, or at the aunt's house only when you know for sure that the aunt will be home the whole time.

It is important to know whom your daughter might encounter when she goes to someone's house. Make sure that you find out from both your daughter and the adult at the home who is *really* around. If you feel self-conscious asking about this kind of information, just think, the other parent or guardian is probably checking you out, too! If you are up-front and open about your household, this will hopefully encourage the other parent or guardian to be just as open.

Action 4: Talk to the parent or guardian and find out information about that person and the rest of the family. Invite them over and get to know them. If something concerns you, rely on your instincts.

Another way that you might gather information about another child and her family is to listen to what other people say about the child and the family. Don't believe everything you hear, and always consider the source, but do keep information in mind if it is concerning. For example, if you are out with the neighborhood parents, you might hear one of the cattier moms in the neighborhood mention, "I heard Cindy was taken away from her mom because her mom was a drug addict. I bet the aunt has some sort of drug problem, too."

This kind of comment is just ignorant all around, but it could potentially sway you if you didn't step back for a moment and reflect. Cindy's mom might have a drug problem; hopefully, if she does, she is getting help for it and she will be healthy enough in the future to be back in her daughter's life. This woman doesn't even know if the aunt has or had a drug issue; she is just making an assumption based on the mother having or having had one. Even if the aunt had a problem with drugs in the past, that doesn't mean she has one now.

You also could ask a trustworthy friend, or your brother Jimmy, who lives in their neighborhood, for information about the family. Perhaps Uncle Jimmy informs you, "They seem like a really nice family, except for the older one. He just got kicked out of some program again and used to get arrested all the time for drinking and having people in and out of the house. I have no idea why his mother puts up with him. I don't think his influence is very good for her niece and nephew." If Uncle Jimmy has always been trustworthy, then what he is telling you is probably pretty reliable. It sounds like he has known the family for a while, and that he is pretty familiar with the situation involving the aunt's son. This doesn't mean your daughter can never hang out with someone who has a member of the family who often gets into trouble; it is just something to be aware of and to take into account when your daughter is going places. You might double check with the aunt and make sure that she is going to be home and will be keeping an eye on the girls when they are there.

Action 5: Listen to "gossip" but do so with an open mind and heart.

So what behaviors are inappropriate? The answer can vary depending on your own comfort zone. A few behaviors that are likely to be considered inappropriate to take part in as a parent include drinking, drugging, letting kids drink or drug, excessive yelling, violence, lying to other parents, and displaying inappropriate sexual behaviors. A parent having a glass of wine after coming home from work is fine. However, it would be pretty concerning to hear from your daughter after she returns from a sleepover that, "Jenny's dad is so funny. He likes to drink wine with Jenny's mom. Sometimes, when they stand up to go to bed, they walk crooked."

How will you learn of these behaviors, if your daughter doesn't tell you? Sometimes you will see these behaviors on display yourself. You may witness a parent who is intoxicated at a school gathering, a parent who swears at a ref at a sporting event and ends up in a fistfight with a parent on the other team, a parent who flirts with all the young girls, or a parent who drives like a maniac all the time.

Unfortunately, you might not hear about these kinds of things until after the fact, but it makes sense to remain alert to them. If a parent drinks excessively at adult parties, believes that it is okay for kids to drink at home as long as they are supervised, is well-known for having huge arguments, or has been caught lying about being at home when he or she wasn't there, these are matters of concern. It is also important to keep in mind what other adults or other children in the household are doing. The parents may be just fine, but perhaps Auntie Julie downstairs likes to tie one on every now and then and wouldn't notice if a bottle of something went missing. An older sibling might think it is fun to let your daughter and her friends take a hit from a joint. Can you plan for every single person who will cross your daughter's path? No. But you can do your best to be aware of who does what in the houses where your daughter visits.

Action 6: Be aware of what inappropriate behaviors other parents may have.

What if you are really uncomfortable with your daughter visiting a certain house?

Maybe she doesn't see the harm in the parents screaming at each other and throwing framed pictures at the walls. You have to be her guide. The safety of your daughter must come before her social needs. As much as she may beg you to go to a party you know won't be supervised, think twice. All it takes is one night where things get out of control and your daughter could end up hurt or worse. If you have heard too many concerning things about a household, listen to your instincts. Give your daughter the opportunity to have the friend come over to your house. You don't need to watch their every move, but be there for them and demonstrate appropriate parental supervision.

What if your daughter goes to a friend's home and realizes that an adult is behaving inappropriately? Before your daughter faces such a situation, have a plan in place for how she can reach you if she doesn't feel safe when she is out. If she is at a home that is close to her house, she can simply leave. If she has a cell phone, she can text you a code word that means come get me, or call me. Let her know that if she is ever in a situation that is scary or dangerous, she can always call the police. Provide her with practice scenarios such as, "What would you do if you were at Tara's house and her older sister came home and didn't seem sober?" Help her come up with answers. She might tell you that she is comfortable just calling you and having you come get her, or she might want to fake that she is sick and then call you to come get her. Make a plan that she is comfortable with and stick to it.

Action 7: Safety comes first. If there is something going on at a friend's house that doesn't seem right to you or your daughter, keep her away from that house. If she goes somewhere and something happens that makes her feel unsafe or uncomfortable, teach her ways of getting out of the situation.

Do you like to drink a little? Do you ever come home buzzed or drunk? What if your daughter is at home with a friend of hers and there is a babysitter with them? Would you consider coming home with a buzz on, since they will probably be in bed when you get home? Think about your own actions and behaviors. Would you be comfortable if your daughter was at a home where the parents were buzzed? You might think, "No, but that is them. When I am buzzed and it is my house, what is the big deal?" The big deal is that your daughter's friend's parents might not be so comfortable with your behavior. Keep that in mind. When your daughter has a friend over, you are charged with the responsibility of taking care of that child. If you are buzzed and you are the only adult in the house, what would happen if your daughter's friend got sick and needed a ride to the hospital? You wouldn't be able to drive her in that state. So think before you engage in inappropriate behaviors. How would you feel if the parent in charge of your daughter for the night was unable to keep her safe?

Are you comfortable with your daughter having her first drink with you? Do you feel that as long as you supervise your daughter and her friends while they drink, then things will be fine? Think again. Not only is that a bad idea, but also it is illegal! Check the laws in your state if you are confused. Allowing your child to drink when she is underage will send a message that drinking is okay with you, and so is breaking the law. Where do you draw the line once you have told her that she can drink at home? What if she starts to take advantage of this and drinks frequently or brings friends over to drink? Don't put yourself in this position. She can wait until she is twenty-one.

Think about your behaviors. Are any of them behaviors you would frown upon if another parent were partaking in one? Do you think that some of your behaviors could be construed as negative? Remember, you are a role model whether you think you are or not. Your daughter and her friends will look to all of the adults around them for guidance and as examples of how they should live their lives. You don't need to be friends with them. You need to help guide them to make good decisions. Be a well-behaved adult that your daughter and her friends can rely on as a safe adult to go to in times of difficulty.

Action 8: Be aware of your own behaviors.

Parents can differ in their beliefs about what is okay when it comes to drinking, drugs, and unsupervised parties. Check in with your daughter and find out how the parents she encounters act. Let her know that she is not at fault if a parent or adult in charge has misbehaved or made a poor choice in supervising. What do you do when you find out an adult has behaved badly? There are a few different options. First, if your daughter relayed the information, thank her for letting you know. It may have been a tough decision for her to tell you. If she tells you, she is acting quite responsibly—which is great! Second, keep your daughter's feelings and concerns in mind. She could be afraid that she will be a social outcast forever if you call the authorities on another parent. This doesn't mean you *shouldn't* do it, but it is something to think about before you do anything rash. Third, verify the information if you can before confronting the parent or getting authorities involved. Maybe another parent that you are close to had a similar experience. Fourth, carefully decide how you will handle the situation. Let's look at how to handle a scenario that comes up quite often.

Danielle asked her mom if she could go to a party at Chrissy's house a week ago. Danielle's mom called Chrissy's mom and asked if she was going to be home. Chrissy's mom said she would be, and not to worry!! Danielle's mom agreed that Danielle could go to the party. Here is what happened:

Danielle and her friend Lisa walked into a party that was pretty busy already. Chrissy's mom walked up to greet them.

"Hi, girls!! There is food in the kitchen and the basement has some items I don't know about. . . . " Chrissy's mom winks at them and walks off.

Danielle and Lisa go to the basement, a bit confused. They find a bunch of their classmates drinking, a keg, and a table with some sort of punch. Chrissy sees them and comes over.

"Hey guys!! The punch is soooooo killer. I think I am drunk already!! Help yourself!"

Danielle looks at Lisa, who looks very uncomfortable.

"Do you want to go? I can call my mom." Danielle says to Lisa.

"Yes, but how lame will we look?"

"We can make something up, like that my mom needed us to babysit my little brother."

"Okay." Lisa looks relived. Danielle takes out her phone and texts her mom a message: Please come get us. We r wicked uncomf. Plz don't ask ?s.

Danielle's mom reads the text and goes back to get the girls.

Danielle and Lisa get in the car. They wave good-bye to Chrissy's mom as she waves to Danielle's mom.

"Are you guys okay?" Danielle's mom asks, concerned.

"Yes. It just wasn't that fun. Jared was there and being mean to Lisa."

"Okay." Danielle's mom lets it go, thinking that Lisa must be upset and she wouldn't want to make her uncomfortable.

The next morning, the mother of another child who went to the party calls Danielle's mom.

"Was Danielle at Chrissy's party last night?"

"Yes, but she only stayed for about fifteen minutes. Why?"

"Well, my daughter told me kids were drinking and that Chrissy's mom knew about it. Will you ask Danielle what she saw?"

Danielle's mom takes a deep breath, "Of course. I will call you back in a bit."

She hangs up the phone and calls for Danielle. Danielle and Lisa both plod down the stairs.

Danielle's mom looks at Danielle and Lisa and reminds herself not to freak out. After all, the girls called for a ride home almost immediately. At least Danielle had the smarts to get out of there and she felt comfortable calling. Okay, maybe there is a little silver lining to this. . . . I could kill Chrissy's mom. What was she thinking??

"Girls, was there drinking going on at the party last night?"

Danielle and Lisa look at one another. Mom chimes in, "This is a safe zone. No punishment to you guys for a parent who is misbehaving."

Danielle nods her head in agreement. "Sorry I didn't tell you, Mom; I just wanted to get out of there."

"I understand, and I am very happy that you made that decision. You can always call me in that sort of situation. There are other parents who heard what was going on. I think we need to either talk to Chrissy's mom or talk to the authorities. I *promise* I will keep you out of it as much as possible. I am going to talk to the other parents about their concerns. Maybe if we all talk, we can come up with a solution that will protect everyone's social life and keep this from ever happening again. What do you say?"

Danielle and Lisa look at each other and shrug. Danielle raises a concern, "Do you promise you will all do this as a group of parents? If you do this alone, everyone is going to hate me and blame me."

"I do appreciate that this could really impact you. I will talk with the other parents and see what they are thinking. I know one thing for sure; I don't want you going back over there. That is a really unsafe situation, and I am not happy she put you in it."

Danielle's mom did get together with the other parents and they approached Chrissy's mom, who felt they were making a big deal out of nothing. There were some parents who wanted to just let it go, but a larger number felt the authorities should know. The group of parents reported it, and the authorities got involved. It did cause some conflict at school. Chrissy and the kids whose parents told basically stayed away from each other, but since there were so many kids whose parents were involved, no one was really on the outs. The only person who did seem to suffer was Chrissy. Although she should have known better as well, it really was Mom who was misbehaving and condoning her daughter's misbehavior.

The great thing about Danielle's mom is that she checked out the story, she didn't rush to punish her daughter, she listened to her daughter's concerns, and she acted firmly and safely.

Action 9: Think carefully about the best way to approach a misbehaving parent.

Chapter 16:
Action Recap

Action 1: Listen carefully to what your daughter tells you about the other adults in her life.

Action 2: Ask her about her new friend, where she lives, and who lives with her.

Action 3: Find out from your daughter what her friend's family is like.

Action 4: Talk to the parent or guardian and find out information about that person and the rest of the family. Invite them over and get to know them. If something concerns you, rely on your instincts.

Action 5: Listen to "gossip" but do so with an open mind and heart.

Action 6: Be aware of what inappropriate behaviors other parents may have.

Action 7: Safety comes first. If there is something going on at a friend's house that doesn't seem right to you or your daughter, keep her away from that house. If she goes somewhere and something happens that makes her feel unsafe or uncomfortable, teach her ways of getting out of the situation.

Action 8: Be aware of your own behaviors.

Action 9: Think carefully about the best way to approach a misbehaving parent.

Chapter 16:
Top Five Talking Points

1. The new girl in your class seems really nice. Do you know her family?

2. I know you think I am nosy and annoying, but I need to make sure the places you go are safe. I would never want anything bad to happen to you.

3. Now that you have been over to her house, what do you think? Is it a safe place to go? Does anyone there do anything that makes you uncomfortable?

4. I hope you know that if an adult is doing something that you don't think is right, you can always tell me and **you** won't get in any trouble for it.

5. Sometimes parents need to make decisions that may seem awful to you, but we do it to make sure that you are as safe as possible. When someone is doing something that puts you at risk, I need to keep you safe.

SEVENTEEN

The Pressure to Achieve

Theresa is tall, blond, the captain of her volleyball team, and in a back-and-forth battle with her best friend to be number one in the class. Theresa sounds like an overachieving high-schooler, but in reality she is a beautiful, brilliant, athletic, kind, miserable, depressed, *seventh-grader*. Theresa came in because her teachers told her parents they were worried about her. She never smiled. Well, she did, but it never seemed real. She smiled to be polite. She smiled when she received a good grade. She smiled when her team won. She never just smiled to smile. She was a bit like a robot. Quite pleasant, but something seemed off.

"Theresa has everything going for her. She is smart, athletic, pretty, nice, you name it! She is a volunteer at a hospital and involved with the farmer's market. She even won the science fair award two years in a row! I can't imagine why her teachers think something is wrong with her. She has Ivy League written all over her," her father protested.

I looked at Theresa and she smiled vacantly back at me. She did have the name of an Ivy League school written on her sweatshirt, but all I saw written all over her was misery. She seemed to feel no enthusiasm at all. Sure, she was happy. She received good grades and she was happy to be the captain of the volleyball team. But none of this seemed to truly inspire her. She didn't learn out of curiosity. She learned to get an A. She didn't play volleyball for the fun of the game. She played to become captain of the team and to win.

"So, Ivy League, huh? Your dad seems to think you will get a full scholarship based on your grades and volleyball."

Theresa smiled, "I sure hope so!"

"What do you think you will study when you go there?"

"I want to be a neurosurgeon or a lawyer."

"Wow!! That is great. What do you like about those jobs?"

Theresa looked puzzled, "I don't know. They seem like good jobs. My parents would be really happy."

"But would you be happy?"

Now the goal of our meeting was not to undermine her parents by any means. It was just to explore what was making Theresa seem so empty, while still encouraging her to do her best.

Months after getting to know her, Theresa still wanted to be a neurosurgeon because she loved science and thought the brain was really cool. She also thought one of the doctors on a popular television show was wicked hot, and figured there must be some good-looking doctors in real life, too. Theresa started paying more attention to why she was interested in different academic subjects instead of just focusing on getting As. She decided volleyball wasn't for her, but she did continue to play for fun. She began running competitively because she really liked it and enjoyed being outside. Being excited about her life didn't make her less of an achiever or less likely to get into college. Instead, it challenged her to appreciate why she wanted to pursue the goals she set for herself. She did change a few of these goals, which enabled her to now work hard for things she enjoys.

Theresa just needed to take a step away from her list of goals and enjoy the journey. That is where the joy is found. The joy isn't always in reaching the finish line, but in enjoying every step along the way to getting there.

Action 1: Take a step back with your daughter and enjoy the moment. Stop focusing on the destination and enjoy the journey.

Pressure is everywhere for our girls—pressure to get the best grades, pressure to pad the college resume, pressure to shoot the most goals, and pressure to perform at an extraordinary level in pretty much everything they try. It is much worse than it was in the past. Nothing seems to be done for pleasure anymore. If your daughter plays soccer, she needs to be the best goalie; if she plays an instrument, she needs to sit first chair; if she is on student government, she'd best be the president. And let's not leave out academic achievement. The pressure to get incredible grades to get into a competitive college is starting at younger and younger ages.

We are so competitive these days that it is a wonder kids have any fun at all. We believe as adults that the better the grades, the better the college; the more activities, the better the scholarship opportunities; the more education, the greater the paycheck; the more money, the more security in life; the more security, the more happiness. So we push them from day one to achieve and to be the best, because we believe that is how to help children succeed.

But what about happiness? It seems parents struggle with this as well. Steven Gross, M.S.W., founder and executive director of Project Joy, points out that "Parents seem to be confused and think that their child's happiness or joy is based on achievement." We always assume if our child loses her soccer game she is sad. If she wins she must be happy. This isn't necessarily true. She may have had a horrible time at her winning game and a super time at her losing game. But we don't allow for this because we don't always ask the right questions or respond in a way that lets our girls express these emotions. We also may give off the impression that we are happy when she wins or disappointed if she loses. Imagine your daughter just got home from her basketball game; here are two different ways to approach the situation:

The Achievement Approach:

"How did your game go?"

"We lost." Your daughter looks frustrated and plops down on the couch.

"Maybe you will win next time."

"Probably not. We stink. It is lame. It isn't fun at all." She gets up and stomps off to her room.

Well, she doesn't sound very joyful.

The Joyful Approach:

"How did your game go?"

"We lost." Your daughter looks frustrated and plops down on the couch.

"Was it fun?"

"Not really. Well, maybe a little. Jenna was there and she is pretty funny. And then while we were shooting around Emily tried to do some crazy shot from the bleachers and she totally missed and hit this guy's Slurpee instead and it was so funny. He even laughed."

"So you had some fun?"

"Yeah, I would miss all the goofy things everyone does if I wasn't there. Plus I really like running around. It feels good to be running around."

Big difference!!! Take the emphasis off the score, and you and your daughter may discover the joy she experiences while at her basketball games.

Steven Gross reminds parents and children every day that joy shouldn't be predicated on whether we win or lose. Joy is this internal sense of wonder and love, and it isn't achieved through external accomplishments. We think that to participate in something, we have to be good at it. That is not true. Think back to when your daughter was a toddler. Maybe she sang at the top of her lungs, kicked a ball around outside, and painted her heart out. And maybe she didn't excel at any of those things, but it didn't matter because she enjoyed them. Let her have joy in her life. Life is really about the balance of striving and achieving your potential, while enjoying the process and remembering to giggle now and then.

Action 2: Remind yourself and your daughter that joy isn't based on achievement. Teach your daughter to balance her drive to achieve with the ability to enjoy the moment.

EDUCATION

Something has changed in education. And the change isn't good. The pressure and stress girls are under to get good grades and to perform at an extraordinary level 100 percent of the time is ridiculous. Why the big change? Isn't this something children shouldn't have to worry about until high school? If only this were true! Elementary school kids are freaking out over their grades and academics. You might think this is a good sign; after all, if they take school seriously, won't they achieve and excel? Not if they have serious anxiety disorders. According to a report from the Surgeon General, almost 21 percent of children between the ages of nine and seventeen have a diagnosable mental health disorder; of these children, 13 percent are diagnosed with an anxiety disorder. That is a lot of anxiety.

Are schools to blame? Not entirely, but there is certainly a great deal of pressure to achieve in school. This is not just in terms of getting into a good college. In many states, students must take state achievement tests to pass to the next grade level or to graduate.

There was even a documentary shown on *60 Minutes* about these tests that shed some frightening light on the pressure felt by students taking the Texas Assessment of Academic Skills (TAAS). An excerpt from the report reads:

> Kids really do worry. Back in Texas, one boy was interviewed by a local reporter on the day before the test.
>
> "When you pass grades, it gets harder and harder, and . . ." said the boy, who then broke into tears.
>
> "Oh my goodness! Is it the interview that's making you nervous?" the reporter asked the boy.
>
> When the boy answered "no," the reporter replied, "No, it's the TAAS that's making you nervous. I'm sorry."

Is this how we want our children experiencing school? No! Should we make sure that they are learning and achieving? Absolutely! But not in a way that creates this much stress. Creating an environment this stressful will only discourage enjoyment in school. Who would want to go somewhere every day where they know they will be filled with anxiety?

Unfortunately for many school districts, the need to achieve has driven out any nonacademic, potentially *fun* classes. Gym, art, music, woodshop, cooking, and most other classes that are not completely academic are often eliminated first when there are budget cuts; in many instances, such classes have already been pared back or eliminated. As a consequence, girls are often missing out on experiencing new activities in school. For many, the school day is packed with English, history, science, math, and little else. Imagine if your daughter is not an academic at heart, how boring and frustrating it must be for her to sit through these classes without a glimpse of other types of learning that may play more to her strengths, enrich her life, and give her a chance to relax.

Learning is important, but it needs to be interesting. It also needs to involve exploration, spark curiosity, and allow for mistakes. Today's kids seem to be driven by grades and scores, instead of by the more natural wonder and curiosity they were born with that should drive learning. They quickly learn in today's day and age that it is the grade, the score, and the result that is important. How do we fix this problem? We fix it by bringing joy back into learning.

This doesn't mean singing a song about multiplication tables, but instead encouraging curiosity in day-to-day activities—including homework. Being curious about something will encourage a child to learn about it because of interest instead of for the carrot at the end of the stick. Schools, parents and guardians, and children all need to work hard to create an interesting learning environment.

Action 3: Encourage your daughter to become curious about her schoolwork and the world around her. Learning is more than just doing work to get it over with or to earn a perfect grade.

EXTRACURRICULARS

Once upon a time, the reason for students to become involved in extracurricular activities was to try things out to figure out what would captivate them. In some cases, such activities also served the function of keeping kids safe by keeping them occupied in productive, structured activities after school. Today, extracurricular activities seem more about padding resumes for the high school or college application process, with the goal of finding something students can excel at in the hopes of improving school choices. Sports, music, theater, clubs—all of these were once done for fun, and were even done during school hours. Many extracurricular activities are now competitive. Most no longer provide opportunities that were available in the past—such as singing off-key but really enjoying it and laughing with a friend who can sing beautifully. Now, if a student can't sing well, she probably won't be allowed to participate; if she does participate, she'd better not hold back the "real" singers from excelling.

Where does this leave the girl who still wants to sing even though she could break glass with her voice? Is her only option to just sing in the shower, or be too embarrassed to sing at all? Learning to win and lose, getting cut from a play, not making a team—these are all very important lessons to learn. There is now not much room for playing for the fun of it; for the most part, kids are in it to win and so are their parents.

As Steven Gross points out: "The biggest thing is for adults to be mindful of what their intention is. It is very hard to do something well if you don't know what your intention is. If your end goal is I want to produce a great soccer player, you are going to push your child to be a great soccer player. If your intention is, I want my child to have fun, and I want to achieve it through soccer, then your practice with your daughter is going to be very different." Gross adds that when parents are unsure of their own intentions this can confuse the child. What is it you are looking for by enrolling your child in an extracurricular activity?

In the same way that it is important to bring joy back into schools, it is important to bring joy back to extracurricular and other activi-

ties as well. Children shouldn't have to excel at something to participate in it. Find an activity where your daughter can go and enjoy
herself, and where there is no pressure. Let her develop skills just for
the fun of it. Allow her the chance to stink or bloom, in an environment where that is okay. Everything doesn't have to be about being
the best.

Action 4: Sign your daughter up for an extracurricular activity that is
stress free, and where she can participate for fun and not for success.

Some girls get it just right. They are able to truly compete at
something while also finding a deep sense of enjoyment in it. But
many cannot compete without feeling so much stress that it seems
to edge out their pleasure. Pushing kids to constantly achieve and
compete exhausts this natural joy, and makes the activity no longer
fun. It doesn't really matter if your daughter excels at something if
she absolutely despises it. Parents often get in the way of this joy by
getting excited, and thinking, "Hmmm. Maybe softball is her thing!
Let's sign her up for every possible softball-related event under the
sun. That way, she can develop into an all-star pitcher and get a
scholarship to college." Such parents for the most part mean well,
but they often get carried away and overdo it. This is another reason
why it is important to stop pushing for perfection. The girl who loves
and excels at softball might not need or want the extra pitching
clinic, the travel team, the all-star team, and her home team. Maybe
she would be just as happy with being on her home team and
enrolling in the pitching clinic. All the additional clinics and teams
might make her feel as though softball was taking over her life, and
not leaving her any time to be with her friends or to have any down
time. It is important for you as a parent to make sure that your
daughter has enough going on to hold her interest, but not so much
that she begins to resent her involvement in activities.

Action 5: Reevaluate how much you encourage your daughter to be involved with activities. Is she involved with too many activities, or too many teams or clinics for one activity? Don't push her so much that she loses her joy.

When we push, we often evaluate. Steven Gross reminds parents that it is important to *notice* how our girls are doing, not just evaluate them all the time. This takes the pressure off. So even if your daughter is involved in a competitive activity, noticing her participation instead of evaluating it is one way to help your daughter see the process and not just the result. Here is an example:

Cheryl was playing in a close volleyball match. She was responsible for four of the points the team scored. Toward the end of the game, the coach switched some players—including Cheryl. She went to her seat on the bench and watched her teammates, cheering them on as they played. The team ended up losing the game, but Cheryl congratulated everyone on her team and on the other team for a job well done. Cheryl's mother reacted:

The Evaluative Way:

"Too bad the team lost! You were doing so well. I don't know why the coach took you out when he did. Those points you scored had the team looking ready to win."

The Noticing Way:

"Hey, you know what I noticed about you today at volleyball? Even when you were sitting on the bench, you were really involved in the game. It seemed like you were really proud of your teammates, too. Did you have fun?"

Does winning and losing matter? Yes, sometimes, but not if your daughter is in a constant state of trying to win or lose, or is totally stressed about trying to win. Try taking the emphasis off evaluation and notice her every day good actions.

Action 6: Take a step back from evaluating your daughter and try noticing her actions.

Does this joy stuff sound a little goofy? Do you have any joy in your own life? Do you remember being a kid and having fun and being joyful? The world has changed for our girls. There is little time for joy unless we help them find it. This doesn't mean pulling them out of activities at which they excel, or letting them slack off at school. We need to show them how to find joy in their lives; if they are not finding joy in their lives, we need to help them find things that will bring joy into their lives. There is joy in just living every day. Even bad days can have some joy in them; it is just a matter of being open to it and giving it the time it deserves.

How can you as a parent teach your daughter how to let joy in? You can do this by making time to be joyful in your own life. Your daughter will learn by your example. Where is your own joy? Are you only motivated by money and success? Ask your daughter if she sees you enjoying yourself or if you are a good, joyful role model? If you want your daughter to find joy, you need to find it within yourself. Steven Gross makes another great point, "You can't spread something you don't have. You can't teach something you don't embody. You have to feel it." Stop what you are doing and enjoy this moment. Enjoy the moment when you are with your daughter. If she is telling you about how interesting the exoskeleton of a beetle is, stop and listen to her. Don't be preoccupied with thoughts of getting her to her lacrosse practice, preparing dinner while she does her homework, and then working on a report for the following day.

Stop. Enjoy the moment. Be present for her. Enjoy her interest in the beetle! You won't get this moment back.

Action 7: Find your own joy and share it with your daughter.

Do you still need convincing that joy is important? Joy does have protective qualities. If you look at the work Steven Gross is doing with Project Joy, it is clear that joy cannot only protect, but it can also heal. Who would want to endure a life that did not have joy? With joy, people are motivated to work through tribulations. Joyful people also attract friends and form healthy social connections, which are extremely protective for kids. If we teach kids early on to be mindful and engaged in the present, it helps them to avoid the anxiety of performance. If they don't need to worry about what comes next, they can enjoy the moment. Anxiety pulls them out of the moment and that is when they start to feel the pressure of needing to achieve. Instill joy in your child's life at an early stage. Joy will only benefit your daughter.

Action 8: Respect joy and its protective qualities.

Chapter 17:
Action Recap

Action 1: Take a step back with your daughter and enjoy the moment. Stop focusing on the destination and enjoy the journey.

Action 2: Remind yourself and your daughter that joy isn't based on achievement. Teach your daughter to balance her drive to achieve with the ability to enjoy the moment.

Action 3: Encourage your daughter to become curious about her schoolwork and the world around her. Learning is more than just doing work to get it over with or to earn a perfect grade.

Action 4: Sign your daughter up for an extracurricular activity that is stress free, and where she can participate for fun and not for success.

Action 5: Reevaluate how much you encourage your daughter to be involved with activities. Is she involved with too many activities, or too many teams or clinics for one activity? Don't push her so much that she loses her joy.

Action 6: Take a step back from evaluating and try noticing.

Action 7: Find your own joy and share it with your daughter.

Action 8: Respect joy and its protective qualities.

Chapter 17:
Top Five Talking Points

1. I know school is really important to you, and it is important to me that you do well. But do you ever just learn out of curiosity or are you always thinking about grades?

2. Is there any time in your day or week that you really enjoy? Do you feel like you do anything just for the fun of it, or is everything goal-oriented?

3. Do you think I am a good example of a person who experiences joy? Why do you think I _____, for fun or for success?

4. I signed you up for a second softball clinic. Now I am wondering if that was such a good idea. Are you getting sick of softball? I want to push you because you are so good at it, but I also want to make sure that you enjoy it, too.

5. Let's go have a catch. It would be really fun to hang outside with you, and just toss a ball back and forth.

CONCLUSION

No book, no course, and no amount of reading or researching will ever prepare you to be a perfect parent or give you the ability to protect your daughter completely from life's dangers. The best you can do is to love her and be there for her when she needs you. Will you make mistakes? Of course. Will she make mistakes? Definitely. Will she face huge obstacles that will scare the heck out of both of you? Yes. But together you will figure it out if you just take the time to do so. Every single person I spoke to in the writing of this book agreed that we all need to take the time to be present for our children. If we are preoccupied, anxious about work, and always in a hurry, then we aren't truly present for our children. It is so difficult to be present for them in today's world that it will take great effort to really be present. But if we do this, we not only become more available to our children, but also, we become role models for them of mindfulness and of being in the moment. Maybe this way, they will live their own lives without all the stress and constant movement in which we are living today. Maybe they will be the generation that says, "Stop. I can only do one thing at a time. I need to be present for this, and I can't do so if I am trying to be perfect and to impress everyone around me."

I hope this book has been helpful. I hope it encourages you to remember that your own childhood wasn't all fun and games. Our girls are growing up much faster than we did. Information is everywhere, and stressors are around every corner. Be the guide your daughter needs to get her through this time. Set a good example. Don't worry so much about what you say; focus on what you do, and listen to what she needs.

CHEAT SHEET

Every now and then a situation may arise where you find yourself wondering, "What on earth do I say now?" Below are some ideas of pretty harmless phrases you can say that won't necessarily fix the problem, but should keep you from making it any worse.

1. "Oh, boy! That is some big news. I need some time to let it sink in. Can we talk about it in a few minutes?" (Go get a glass of water, hyperventilate, and collect yourself.)

2. "I love you very much."

3. "Maybe you can help me understand what is going on. I know _____'s side of the story, but what is your take on it?"

4. "I hear you. I do. I am listening to you, and I will take that into consideration when making my decision."

5. "I know that is not the decision you wanted to hear, but I have to make a decision based on what I believe is best and safest for you. I am sorry you don't agree with it, but after taking all sides into consideration, that is my decision."

6. "You are right. I have no idea how it feels to be you, but I do imagine that you are frustrated with me. I am sorry you feel that way, but everything I do really is out of love and concern for your well-being."

7. "It seems like you are in a pretty tough spot right now. Is there anything I can do that would make it any easier?"

8. "_____ is not the be-all-end-all of life. I know it feels like it is right now, but I promise you it isn't. There is so much more, and the feelings you have right now are awful and very real, but they are temporary. Even though I am an old fart in your book, I was once a kid like you and I promise that life will get better."

9. "Being a kid is pretty tough. I want to make things as happy and as safe for you as I can."

10. "I love you when I am angry, I love you when I am sad, I loved you yesterday, I love you now, and I will love you tomorrow."

TOP TWELVE TO REMEMBER WHEN TALKING TO YOUR DAUGHTER

1 No matter what goes on between you and your daughter, remind her often and especially in times of difficulty that you love her. Teach her that being angry with her doesn't mean you no longer love her or that you love her any less. She is going to mess up; she is going to go through tough times and fabulous times. Through all of these times, you will love her.

2 Before you react to anything in anger, take pause. Let it sink in, get your head on straight, and then respond. This could take minutes, or it could take hours. There is no harm in saying, "Boy, this is big news. I need some time to think about it." Take the time you need to figure out how to best approach a difficult situation. There is no harm in taking some time to get your head on straight.

3 DO NOT SAY, "You have no idea how hard it is to be an adult. You are so lucky to be a kid." While it is true, it is only true in hindsight. If we could go back to being kids knowing what we know now, we would appreciate being kids and having parents who take care of us. When you are a kid, however, you have no comprehension of this, and muddling through things like puberty, school, and

social issues for the first time is incredibly difficult. Do any of us *really* want to repeat fifth grade or junior high?? Appreciate what she is going through. Your life as an adult is tough, too, but find someone else to sympathize with you, not your twelve-year-old who just failed her English quiz and found out her BFF was text messaging the boy she likes.

4 "Save the drama for your mama." You and everyone else will get the drama, and probably a lot of it! Her emotional mind is in control of her brain right now. Of course she is going to be a drama queen! Don't yell at her or be angry with her. Teach her how to balance her emotions. She needs to learn how to see things with a rational mind, not just an emotional one. Validate her feelings, appreciate her feelings, and then help her get a grip and see beyond whatever drama has consumed her.

5 Appreciate that you *do not* know what it is like to be her or to be a kid growing up in today's world. You really don't. She doesn't know what it was like to grow up in your time. Maybe it was harder, maybe it was easier. It doesn't matter; it isn't a competition. Growing up is tough for everyone. Be there to support her. Learn about her world from your daughter and her friends. Don't pretend to know it all when you don't. Let them teach you.

6 Think she hates you? She might. Take it as a compliment. As girls grow up, it is often easier for them to separate from the person around whom they feel safest if they hate them or get mad at them. It is hard for girls to find their independence. For them to do so, they often push their moms away. To ease the heartache you might feel over this, remind yourself that she is probably doing it because she loves you so much that it is too hard for her to grow into

her own woman while staying super close to you. As unwanted as your daughter may make you feel, she needs you more than ever, so be there for her even more on the days when she tells you she hates you.

7 Fess up when you make a mistake. Say, "Oops, that was my mistake. I'm sorry I blamed that on you. It really was your brother who took the car. Sorry, sweetie." Teaching her that it is better to admit that you made a mistake than to lie or get defensive about it will help her admit to and learn from her own mistakes.

8 Stop expecting perfection from yourself, your daughter, or from anyone. How boring would we be without imperfection? Lead by example. Stop trying to do it all, and encourage her to chill out now and then. She doesn't have to be perfect all the time—or ever!

9 Fake it till you make it. Sometimes, you might have to lie. If your daughter is facing a big issue, and she needs to hear that things will be okay, you can lie. She needs to know you will keep her safe, and be there for her. Things will be okay eventually—even if it's not in the way you or she wanted everything to be.

10 Shush. Be quiet. Listen to her. Really listen. It is so important that you listen to the jibberish, sadness, anger, fear, and silence. You don't have to fix them all of the time. Sometimes, all she needs is to know that you are there to listen to her—without judgment and without a story about your own childhood. Just be there to listen.

11 Be her partner, not her dictator. Ask her opinion, and include her in decisions that impact her life. You may disagree and ultimately make a decision that isn't thrilling for her, but ask for and pay attention to her input.

12 You cannot plan for how her life can go. You can lead her, guide her, support her, help her, but you cannot plan her life for her. Experience the bumps, twists, and turns of her life with her, and help her find the joy in them—no matter how difficult and unpredictable they might be.

REFERENCES

American Council for Drug Education, "Signs and Symptoms of Drug Use." Available from http://www.acde.org/parent/signs.htm (accessed June 15, 2010).

Bronson, Po, and Ashley Merryman. *NurtureShock*. New York, NY.: Twelve, 2009. Chapter 9, pages 184–185.

Canadian Press, The. 2007. Uplifting Story of the Bra. Available from http://news.therecord.com/Life/article/281978 (accessed June 15, 2010).

Equal Rights Advocates, "Sexual Harassment at School: Know Your Rights." Available from http://www.equalrights.org/publications/kyr/shschool.asp (accessed June 15, 2010).

Evenson, Ranae J., and Robin W. Simon. 2005. Clarifying the Relationship Between Parenthood and Depression. *Journal of Health and Social Behavior* 46 (4): 341–58, http://hsb.sagepub.com/cgi/content/abstract/46/4/341 (accessed June 15, 2010).

JumpStart Coalition for Personal Financial Literacy, "Home page." Available from http://www.jumpstart.org/ (accessed June 15, 2010).

Kantrowitz, Barbara. 2009. Coming-of-Age Stories. Available from http://www.newsweek.com/2009/01/27/coming-of-age-stories.html (accessed June 15, 2010).

LD Online, "What Is a Learning Disability?" Available from http://www.ldonline.org/ldbasics/whatisld (accessed June 15, 2010).

National Inhalant Prevention Coalition, "Frequently Asked Questions." Available from http://www.inhalants.org/faqs.htm (accessed June 15, 2010).

National Institute of Child Health and Human Development, "Puberty." Available from http://www.nichd.nih.gov/health/topics/puberty.cfm (accessed June 15, 2010).

National Institute on Alcohol Abuse and Alcoholism, 2006. Underage Drinking: Why Do Adolescents Drink, What Are the Risks, and How Can Underage Drinking Be Prevented? *Alcohol Alert 67,* http://pubs.niaaa.nih.gov/publications/AA67/AA67.htm (accessed June 15, 2010).

National Youth Violence Prevention Resource Center, "Bullying Facts and Statistics." Available from http://www.safeyouth.org/scripts/faq/bullying.asp (accessed June 15, 2010).

60 Minutes, 2000. Texas Test Two-Step. Available from http://www.cbsnews.com/stories/2000/09/10/60minutes/main232069.shtml (accessed June 15, 2010).

Springer, 2008. Sexual Harassment at School—More Harmful than Bullying. *ScienceDaily* (April 24), http://www.sciencedaily.com/releases/2008/04/080423115922.htm (accessed June 15, 2010).

Substance Abuse and Mental Health Services Administration, "Children's Mental Health Facts: Children and Adolescents with Anxiety Disorders." Available from http://mentalhealth.samhsa.gov/publications/allpubs/ca-0007/default.asp#8 (accessed June 15, 2010).

Substance Abuse and Mental Health Services Administration, "Talk Early, Talk Often, Get Others Involved." Available from http://www.underagedrinking.samhsa.gov/ (accessed June 15, 2010).

Surgeon General, "Mental Health: A Report of the Surgeon General." Available from http://www.surgeongeneral.gov/library/mentalhealth/chapter3/sec1.html (accessed June 15, 2010).

U.S. Equal Employment Opportunity Commission, "Facts About Sexual Harassment." Available from http://www.eeoc.gov/eeoc/publications/fs-sex.cfm (accessed June 15, 2010).

Wang, Jing, Ronald J. Iannotti, and Tonja R. Nansel. 2009. School Bullying Among Adolescents in The United States: Physical, Verbal, Relational, and Cyber. *Journal of Adolescent Health* 45 (4): 368–75.

CONTRIBUTORS

Steven Gross, M.S.W., is the founder and executive director of Project Joy, a nonprofit organization that uses play to strengthen and heal children whose lives have been deeply impacted by trauma. He has devoted his career to the service of our most vulnerable children. A pioneer in utilizing exuberant, joyful play to promote resiliency in children and a leader in the field of psychological trauma response, Gross is committed to the healthy development of children facing the most unfair circumstances.

Elizabeth Driscoll Jorgensen, CADC, is a substance abuse counselor and owner of Insight Counseling, in Ridgefield, Connecticut, specializing in the treatment of adolescents and young adults.

Anne Townsend, Ph.D., is the executive director and lead instructor at Mariposa Child Success Programs, where she is also a parent coach. Dr. Townsend holds a Ph.D. in family science from the University of Maryland and an M.S. in psychology. She has more than twelve years of experience working with parents, teachers, child care workers, and therapists in Maryland and has taught classes at the University of Maryland and Baltimore City Community College. Her research focuses on the impact that parents and teachers have on child success outcomes such as academic achievements, social competencies, and physical health. Dr. Townsend has created and implemented all of the programs at Mariposa.

Harriette E. Wimms, Ph.D., is the director of community outreach and a lead instructor at Mariposa Child Success Programs. She is also a faculty member in the divisions of pediatric psychology and neuropsychology at Mt.

Washington Pediatric Hospital and provides therapeutic services and training to children, families, and professionals. For more than fifteen years she has worked with children, families, schools, and community agencies throughout Baltimore City to improve the interpersonal, emotional, and academic outcomes for children living in impoverished communities. A former Meyerhoff Scholar, Dr. Wimms holds a Ph.D. in psychology from the University of Maryland, Baltimore County, and has received specialty training in the areas of child clinical psychology and community/social psychology. She also holds an M.S. in developmental psychology from Johns Hopkins University. Committed to improving educational outcomes for Baltimore City children, she is a founder of the Baltimore Montessori Public Charter School and has served on the board of the Children of the World (early learning co-op).

INDEX

ABOUT THE AUTHOR

ERIN A. MUNROE is the author of *The Everything Guide to Stepparenting,* technically reviewed by Irene Levine, Ph.D., and published by Adams Media. She has also authored *The Anxiety Workbook for Girls* for Fairview Press. Currently, Erin works as a licensed mental health counselor at the South Boston Community Health Center where she sees children, adolescents, and families experiencing a range of issues, including trauma, substance abuse, depression, anxiety, attention deficit disorders, adjustment disorders, and more. Erin's position at the health center started as a part-time position in the confidential teen clinic where Erin still provides counseling and support to teenagers struggling with anything from college applications to talking to their parents about pregnancy. Erin has been working in the mental health field since 2001 and has primarily worked with adolescents in schools as a licensed school guidance counselor and adjustment counselor and outside of school as a licensed mental health counselor. She found her way into the field after working with a program whose goal it was to reunite families whose children had been taken away due to abuse and neglect. A great portion of this job was dedicated to educating families on how to be the best parents they could be. The rewarding part was watching parents and guardians implement these strategies and gain success as a family unit. Following this experience, Erin attended Boston University where she earned her degree in mental health counseling and behavioral medicine. Prior to earning her graduate degree, Erin attended the College of the Holy Cross where she majored in English and completed significant coursework in deaf studies.

Erin also provides trainings in self care, relaxation, life balance, how to understand your daughter's anxiety, and identifying and managing mental illness in the classroom.